THE
CIVIL
WAR

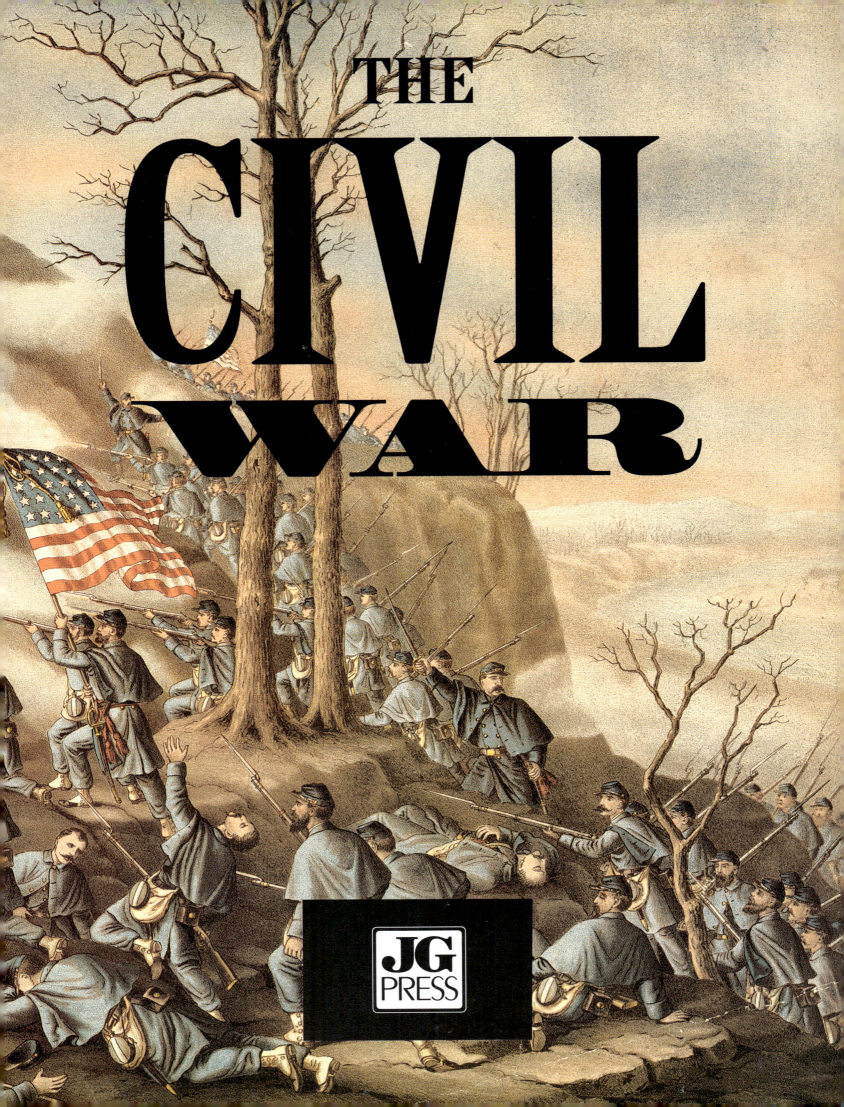

THE
CIVIL
WAR

JG
PRESS

Published in the USA 1997 by JG Press
Distributed by World Publications, Inc.

The JG Press imprint is a trademark of
JG Press, Inc.
455 Somerset Avenue
North Dighton, MA 02764

Produced by
Brompton Books Corporation
15 Sherwood Place
Greenwich, Connecticut 06830

ISBN 1–57215–239–7

Printed in China

Page 1: A massive 15-inch Rodman gun,
part of the Army of the Potomac's outer
defenses of Washington, DC.

Pages 2-3: The Battle of Lookout
Mountain (November 24, 1863), as
rendered by Kurz & Allison.

This page: A painting by Edwin Forbes
shows the view from the summit of Little
Round Top on July 3, 1863, the final day of
the Battle of Gettysburg.

CONTENTS

INTRODUCTION

Professional and amateur historians have always been fascinated by the Civil War, but in recent years the general public has expressed unusually strong interest in it as well. Ken Burns's extraordinary documentary on the war, viewed on public television and videocassette by millions of people, certainly heightened the public's curiosity about this crucial period in American history. But interest had been building for several years before the documentary first aired.

One reason for the resurgence of interest may be that the story of the Civil War speaks to a collective yearning in twentieth-century America for a new set of national values – a moral framework and a sense of community. Given this yearning, it is perhaps only natural that we should be drawn to a period in which Americans sacrificed their lives for such concepts as honor, freedom and national unity.

To be sure, the Civil War was not a purely idealistic conflict. America in the mid-nineteenth century was certainly a materialistic nation, and one might argue that the war was largely a struggle between greedy capitalists on one side and greedy slave-owners on the other. But the conflict was also about America's most fundamental principles. And it was fought by men and women who sincerely and passionately believed that *their* interpretation of these principles – their concept of a just and free society – was morally sound.

On another level, the war is fascinating simply as drama. Ironic details abound: boys of the North and the South butchering each other on the battlefield, then calling an unofficial truce and chatting casually while sharing coffee, tobacco and newspapers; Wilmer McClean, fleeing his home in Manassas, Viriginia, to escape the war – only to have Grant and Lee land in his front parlor in Appomattox four years later; "Stonewall" Jackson, who might well have turned the tide for the South, dying from a bullet wound inflicted accidentally by one of his own men; a young Rebel risking his life after the Battle of Fredericksburg to bring water to his dying enemies. This is the stuff of fiction, yet it happened.

Again, the war is like no other because it came at a time when America was crossing the threshold from an agricultural to a modern industrial society. In some ways, particularly for the South, it was an old-fashioned war, a war in which, for instance, horsemanship played an important role. As a result, certain images from the war strike us as romantic. But in other ways the Civil War was the first truly modern military conflict, a fact that is reflected both in the harsh military strategies and tactics of Grant and Sherman and in the new technologies that played key roles in the conflict.

Certainly one of those innovations – photography – has much to do with our present-day interest in the war. The fact that we have an extensive visual record of the conflict allows us to appreciate many things that could never be so powerfully conveyed in words. It is one thing to read descriptions of battles; it is another to look at a photograph of a wide-eyed corpse on a battlefield. No written account of slavery can produce quite the same effect as the photographic image of a slave whose back is a mass of scar tissue raised by repeated whippings. And even looking into the young-old faces in those apparently mundane pictures of Yankees and Rebels in their respective camps can be singularly moving.

This book presents an exceptionally large selection of photographs from the war, but it is not solely photographic simply because many key events were never captured on camera. The technology was, after all, relatively new and still quite cumbersome. (Field photography became practical only around 1851.) Therefore, in addition to photographs, the book includes reproductions of Civil War art: pictures ranging from pencil sketches to formal oil paintings. Many of the sketches, drawn by leading American artists such as Winslow Homer, are rough, since they were done on the battlefield. But because they evoke such a strong sense of immediacy, they are often more powerful than finished paintings. Moreover, the sketches are interesting because they became the basis for engravings that appeared in major publications of the day. As such, they helped to shape Americans' perceptions of the war as it was unfolding.

The text in this book is intended to place the pictures into their historical context, but it is not intended to be a comprehensive narrative. The primary focus of the book is the pictures themselves. They have a powerful story to tell.

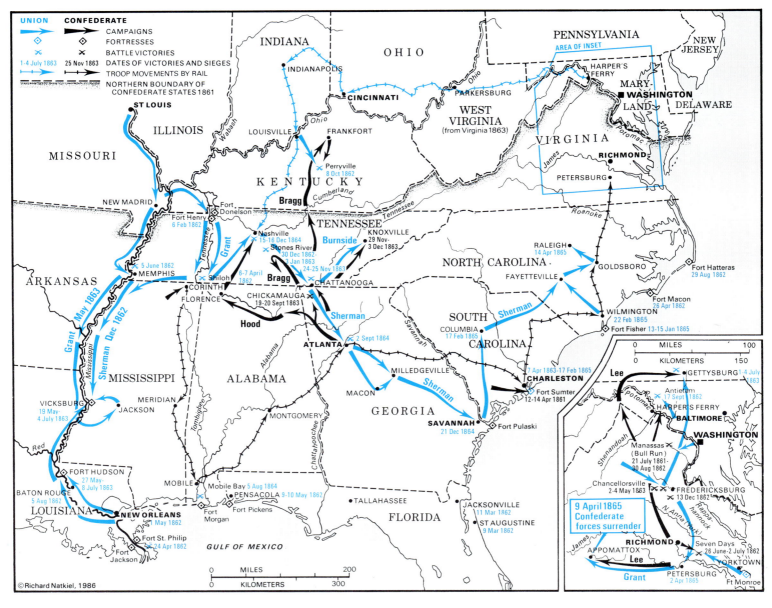

UNION	CONFEDERATE	
→	→	CAMPAIGNS
◇	◇	FORTRESSES
✕	✕	BATTLE VICTORIES
1-4 July 1863	25 Nov 1863	DATES OF VICTORIES AND SIEGES
⇒	➤	TROOP MOVEMENTS BY RAIL
		NORTHERN BOUNDARY OF CONFEDERATE STATES 1861

© Richard Natkiel, 1986

MILES 0 — 200
KILOMETERS 0 — 300

MILES 0 — 100
KILOMETERS 0 — 150

Opposite: A Union battery reloads during the attack on Fredericksburg in 1863. This photograph, from the Mathew Brady Collection, was the first to actually show American troops in the midst of battle.

Above: The major campaigns of the war.

Right: Casualties in the Battle of Corinth, Miss. This photograph was taken the evening of Oct. 4, 1862. Several weeks later the New York *Times* commented, "M. Brady has done something to bring home to us the terrible reality and earnestness of war. If he has not brought bodies and laid them in our door-yards and along our streets, he has done something very like it."

PROLOGUE: PRELUDE TO WAR

America in the mid-nineteenth century was a land of seemingly unlimited potential. We need only look at the magnificent landscape paintings of the period to get a sense of the exhilaration many white Americans must have felt as they pondered the future of this rich, vast continent and speculated about how it ultimately would be transformed.

Much of the land, of course, had already been developed. By 1850 the United States had 9000 miles of railroad — more than any other nation in the world. Canals and all-weather roads had also been built at an unprecedented pace, while the recently-invented telegraph further accelerated the coming of the modern age. All of these developments spurred the growth of cities. While the country remained predominately rural at mid-century, the urban population grew three times faster than the rural population between 1810 and 1860. Overall, the population quadrupled during this period.

Accompanying this rapid growth was the acquisition of expansive new territories, most recently from Mexico. These territories provided extraordinary new opportunities for individuals and for the country as a whole. Before the opportunities could be fully exploited, however, Americans had to come to terms with their sharply conflicting visions of the future.

For most Northerners the future lay in industrial capitalism. But not all Northerners whole-heartedly embraced this new economic system, for the dark side of capitalism in America had already been revealed: craftsmanship had been replaced to a large extent by the factory system, which was oppressively regimented for many workers. But the factory system was also undeniably the key to rapid economic growth, and proponents of the system argued that free (*i.e.*, wage) labor and industrial capitalism gave every American the chance to rise as high as his talents and determination would take him.

Southerners, for the most part, held a drastically different vision of the future, and Southern society at mid-century reflected this. While Northerners were developing a versatile, industrial economy, the South was becoming increasingly dependent on agriculture in general and cotton in particular. Some Southerners were painfully aware that the region lagged behind the North in every area of modern development, from transportation and manufacturing to education and communications. But the paramount concern for most Southerners was the preservation of traditions. "Progress," as Northerners defined it, would no doubt undermine those traditions.

"We have no cities," said one Alabama politician, "and we don't want them. . . . We desire no trading, no mechanical, or manufacturing classes. As long as we have our rice, our sugar, our tobacco, and our cotton, we can command wealth to purchase all we want."

The crucial element the politician failed to mention was, of course, slavery. Not that mid-century Southerners were apologetic about the institution, as many of their ancestors had been. What once had been regarded as a "necessary evil" had now become, in the eyes of most Southerners, a

CAUTION!!

COLORED PEOPLE

OF BOSTON, ONE & ALL,

You are hereby respectfully CAUTIONED and advised, to avoid conversing with the

Watchmen and Police Officers of Boston,

For since the recent ORDER OF THE MAYOR & ALDERMEN, they are empowered to act as

KIDNAPPERS

AND

Slave Catchers,

And they have already been actually employed in KIDNAPPING, CATCHING, AND KEEPING SLAVES. Therefore, if you value your LIBERTY, and the *Welfare of the Fugitives* among you, *Shun* them in every possible manner, as so many *HOUNDS* on the track of the most unfortunate of your race.

Keep a Sharp Look Out for KIDNAPPERS, and have TOP EYE open.

APRIL 24, 1851.

force for good. Southerners argued that plantation slaves were better off, in terms of basic needs, than the miserable, impoverished wage laborers of the North. Furthermore, the institution of slavery allowed white men (at least those who were wealthy enough to own slaves) to live leisurely, cultivated, and "chivalrous" lives – a concept of life that was firmly rooted in Southern culture.

Committed to an economy that required vast amounts of land, Southerners became the driving force behind the acquisition of new territories. And since slavery was inextricably linked with this economy, not to mention Southern culture, Southerners were not about to accept restrictions on whether new territories should be "slave" or "free".

Restrictions were exactly what most Northern politicians had in mind. While few Northerners were abolitionists, more opposed the expansion of slavery on moral grounds and more still because it violated the Puritan work ethic, which was part of their heritage, and because it undermined the free-labor ideology, which had become the basis of their society. Thus a young Congressman from Pennsylvania could call for the prohibition of slavery in all territories acquired from Mexico not out of "morbid sympathy for the slave . . . The negro race already occupies enough of this fair continent," but to preserve the new territories for "free white labor." In the end, however, motivations did not matter. It was the opposition to the expansion of slavery that counted.

In 1850 Congress passed a series of compromises hoping to keep the conflict over slavery in check. In some ways the compromise bills had the opposite effect. One of the bills admitted California as a free state, while another established a strict new fugitive slave law. Together, the bills infuriated both Northerners and Southerners.

The Fugitive Slave Act was particularly divisive. Initially, many moderate and conservative Northerners urged compliance with the law, which required Northern states to return escaped slaves to their Southern masters. In 1854, however, the law took on a human face, and opposition to it grew. On May 24 of that year slave catchers seized Anthony Burns, a Virginia slave who had escaped to Boston. Since Burns had become a working member of the community and many Bostonians had come to know him, his arrest struck residents of the city as a threat to liberty in general. Aboli-

tionists attempted to free him by force but failed. Then city leaders, sensing massive support for Burns, attempted to buy his freedom. The Pierce Administration refused and sent in federal troops to escort him back to Virginia. One local politician summed up the transformation in the community as a result of the incident: "We went to bed one night old fashioned conservatives," he wrote, "and waked up stark mad Abolitionists."

That same year, passage of the Kansas-Nebraska Act aggravated the conflict over slavery on a much broader scale. The Act violated the Missouri Compromise by allowing popular will to determine the future of slavery in areas where it had previously been banned. When it came time to elect a territorial government in Kansas, pro-slavery forces poured in from Missouri to tip the balance in their favor. Anti-slavery settlers urged the Pierce Administration to invalidate the fraudulent election, but the President refused. Subsquently, anti-slavery settlers held a new election, and Kansas was left with two separate governments. Sporadic violence and rioting followed, and the area came to be known as "Bleeding Kansas."

Back in Washington, Massachusetts Senator Charles Sumner was among those who were infuriated by the "rape" of Kansas. In particular, he castigated Senator Andrew Butler from South Carolina. Two days later Butler's cousin assaulted Sumner in the Senate chamber, repeatedy beating him over the head with a cane. The assault was widely celebrated in South Carolina as a necessary defense of honor. Northerners, of course, denounced it just as vehemently as a barbaric act.

In 1857 pro-slavery forces won another important victory: the Dred Scott Decision. Dred Scott, a Missouri slave, had sued for freedom on the grounds that his master had taken him into the free state of Illinois and into Wisconsin territory, where slavery had been barred by the Missouri Compromise. The case worked its way up to the Supreme Court, and on March 6 the Court announced its decision, which was written by Chief Justice Roger Taney. Taney had gone far beyond the question at hand, asserting that blacks in general were "beings of an inferior order. . . . so far inferior, that they had no rights which the white man was bound to respect." He further ruled that the Missouri Compromise was unconstitutional. The ruling infuriated anti-slavery Northerners

Opposite, far left: A Currier & Ives lithograph mocks President Buchanan, right, for failing to stand firm against secessionists who were threatening Fort Sumter. Having refused to withdraw his troops, he regarded the Southern attack on a reinforcement vessel on January 9 1861 as an act of war.

Left: An 1851 poster warning blacks about a new ordinance empowering local police to act as slave catchers.

Right: Civilians and members of the militia rush toward Harper's Ferry after receiving word of John Brown's raid on the Federal arsenal on October 16, 1859.

Above and left: A planter's house on the Mississippi and slaves picking cotton in Alabama. The invention of the cotton gin just before the turn of the century had made growing cotton economically viable. Southern plantations doubled their cotton output each decade between 1800 and 1860. In the process, they became increasingly dependent on this single crop and the slaves who picked it.

Opposite, left: Roger Taney, Chief Justice of the Supreme Court from 1836 to 1864 and writer of the Dred Scott Decision.

Opposite, right: An illustration from *Uncle Tom's Cabin.* Published in serial form in 1851, the book caused an uproar in both the North and the South for its depiction of the cruelties of slavery.

because it theoretically opened all territories to slavery and implied that slave owners could even bring their slaves into free states for an indefinite period.

A year after the Dred Scott Decision, Abraham Lincoln and Stephen Douglas distilled the debate over slavery during their campaign for the Senate. At the close of the convention which nominated Lincoln, the future President gave his famous "House Divided" speech: "I believe this government cannot endure, permanently half slave and half free," he said. "I do not expect the Union to be dissolved . . . but I do expect it will cease to be divided. . . . Either opponents of slavery will arrest the further spread of it. . . . or advocates will push it forward, till it shall become alike lawful in all States, old as well as new – North as well as South." Lincoln lost the election but in the process established himself as an important, if moderate, anti-slavery voice. By 1860 he would gain enough prominence to win the six-year-old Republican Party's nomination for the Presidency and would then go on to win the election from the badly split Democrats.

Meanwhile the country's most extreme radical on the issue of slavery had put his own plans into effect. Most people who knew of John Brown's plan to incite a slave uprising – including Frederick Douglass and others who shared Brown's goal of abolition – recognized it as a poor one. Nonetheless, on the night of October 16, 1859, Brown and 23 others attacked the federal arsenal at Harper's Ferry with the ultimate objective of arming slaves and sparking a widespread rebellion. The band captured the arsenal, but citizens and militia surrounded Brown and his men. That night Marines, led by Colonel Robert E. Lee, arrived on the scene, and the following morning they stormed the building. Tactically, Brown's raid had been a failure, but if his strategy was to galvanize anti-slavery sentiment, he succeeded. Two weeks after the raid he was sentenced to hang – a sentence he accepted without flinching. In willingly sacrificing his life for the cause of abolition Brown became a martyr and drew admiration from many Northerners. At the same time, more and more Southerners talked openly of succession, in part because they feared that further agitation might indeed incite a revolt among slaves.

The following year, the year of the Presidential election, the Union finally fell apart. Lincoln's personal moderation notwithstanding, the repellent prospect of a Republican in the White House was more than most traditional Southerners could bear. By December 20 South Carolina had seceded, and by February six other states had also broken from the Union.

In the wake of the secessionist conventions many Southerners expressed confidence that Yankees would not fight. Had secession occurred a decade earlier they might have been right, but during the 1850s much had occurred to solidify anti-slavery and anti-Southern feelings in the North. The prediction that John Brown had made just before walking to the gallows proved to be right. "I . . . am now quite certain," he wrote in a farewell note, "that the crimes of this guilty land will never be purged away but with Blood."

"As far as I can judge from the papers we are between a state of anarchy & Civil war. May God avert us from both."
Robert E. Lee, January, 1861

On January 21, 1861, Jefferson Davis withdrew from the Senate in support of Mississippi's vote to secede. That night he went home and prayed for peace. Davis's mood that day was shared by much of the nation early in 1861. The Civil War had not yet begun on the battlefield, but Americans, North and South, were solemnly preparing themselves for an explosive struggle, even though they feared it.

Not all Americans were torn by such inner conflict, of course. The hearts of many had long since been saturated with hatred. They wanted war – and perhaps needed it as a catharsis. But throughout the winter of 1861 many leaders expressed the belief that war could be avoided, even if they knew it was inevitable. "There needs to be no bloodshed or violence," said Lincoln upon his first inauguration in March. "We are not enemies. . . ."

But by the following month all was lost. When South Carolina artillery fired on Fort Sumter, and Lincoln issued his call for 75,000 troops to put down the "insurrection," the voices of compromise fell silent. "There can be no neutrals in this war, only patriots – or traitors," Stephen Douglas told Lincoln. Likewise, Unionist sympathies in the South had been "wiped out of existence," according to one observer.

Still, the bombardment of Sumter had not killed a single man on either side, and no American could have imagined in the spring of 1861 the "total war" that was to come. As each side scrambled to organize armies, many Americans expressed a belief that the war would be short.

This was the prevailing sentiment in July when Northern civilians gathered for a Sunday outing to watch the Yankees whip the Rebels near Manassas Junction in northern Virginia. But the afternoon's entertainment turned out to be shockingly different from what the spectators had expected. The surprise Southern victory at the First Battle of Bull Run thrust into the faces of soldiers and civilians alike the complexity and horror of war. Americans were gradually coming to the realization that the conflict might not end so quickly after all.

Whatever its duration, most Northerners agreed, the war should be fought to preserve the Union – not to end slavery – and on July 25 Congress voted 30 to 5 in favor of a resolution to that effect. Having endorsed this political stance for the North, Lincoln began casting about for the military leadership that could lead the Union to victory.

A week after the defeat at Bull Run, Lincoln appointed a dashing and supremely confident 34-year-old, George B. McClellan, to the command of the Army of the Potomac. Four months later McClellan replaced General Winfield Scott – 40 years his senior – as general in chief of the Union Army. Given the army's profound lack of discipline, the appointment made sense. McClellan was highly skilled at military organization and commanded a great deal of respect among the troops. Later, of course, he would reveal his fundamental inability to command effectively on the battlefield. But for now, Northerners embraced him as a savior.

Previous pages: Abraham Lincoln delivers his masterly inaugural address on the steps of the unfinished Capitol. "There needs to be no bloodshed or violence," Lincoln said, ". . . We are not enemies. The mystic chords of memory, stretching from every battlefield and patriot grave to every living heart and hearthstone all over this broad land, will yet swell the chorus of the Union when [it] is again touched . . . by the better angels of our nature."

Left: A patriotic painting published early in the war.

Opposite top: The *Sumter*, a blockade runner, eludes the Union ship *Brooklyn* in the summer of 1861.

Right: The bombardment of Fort Sumter.

THE UNION IS DISSOLVED

Opposite: William Lloyd Garrison, a leading abolitionist, who called the Republican Party "cowardly" for endorsing restriction of slavery rather than abolition.

Above: Lincoln visits the House of Representatives several weeks before his inauguration. The *Illustrated News* stated that the visit was "without precedent in the history of the Kings of America."

Far left: Jefferson Davis, passionate advocate for the Southern way of life ever since his election to the House of Representatives in 1845. He was opposed to secession throughout 1860, but once his state left the Union on January 21, 1861, he resigned from the Senate. Three weeks later he was elected provisional President of the Confederate States of America.

Left: Frederick Douglass, a former slave who became a leading abolitionist. In January 1861 he wrote: "If the Union can only be maintained by new concessions to the slaveholders, if it can only be stuck together . . . by a new drain on the negro's blood, then . . . let the Union perish."

Opposite: Jefferson Davis is inaugurated in front of the Alabama State Capitol in Montgomery. With Davis at the podium are Alex H. Stephens, Vice President of the Confederacy, William L. Yancey, a leader of the secession movement, and Howell Cobb, president of the Confederate Senate. The Confederate capital was later moved to Richmond. This illustration was copied from a photograph taken at the time.

Above: The last hours of Congress, March 1859. The voices of compromise steadily diminished between 1859 and 1861; nonetheless, right up until the firing on Fort Sumter there were those who held out hope for a political solution to the conflict.

Right: A special edition of the Charleston (South Carolina) *Mercury* announces passage of the state's secession ordinance on December 20, 1860. "The tea has been thrown overboard," the paper stated. "The revolution of 1860 has been initiated." Despite the militant rhetoric, however, the paper's editor, Barnwell Rhett, was among many prominent Southerners who did not anticipate a civil war resulting from secession.

CHARLESTON MERCURY

EXTRA:

Passed unanimously at 1.15 o'clock, P. M. December 20th, 1860.

AN ORDINANCE

To dissolve the Union between the State of South Carolina and other States united with her under the compact entitled "The Constitution of the United States of America."

We, the People of the State of South Carolina, in Convention assembled, do declare and ordain, and it is hereby declared and ordained,

That the Ordinance adopted by us in Convention, on the twenty-third day of May, in the year of our Lord one thousand seven hundred and eighty-eight, whereby the Constitution of the United States of America was ratified, and also, all Acts and parts of Acts of the General Assembly of this State, ratifying amendments of the said Constitution, are hereby repealed; and that the union now subsisting between South Carolina and other States, under the name of "The United States of America," is hereby dissolved.

THE UNION IS DISSOLVED!

FORT SUMTER

Above: The interior of Fort Sumter after Union surrender of the fort on April 14, 1861. The previous February, the Confederate provisional Congress had resolved to take Sumter and other forts as early as possible, "either by negotiation, or force." Meanwhile, supplies at the fort were quickly dwindling. Secretary Seward and others recommended against reinforcement of the fort, fearing that such a move would precipitate war. Lincoln ultimately decided to send supplies in unarmed transports; troops and warships would stand by in case of Confederate attack. He notified Jefferson Davis of his intentions, thus laying responsibility for starting or avoiding war in the lap of the Confederacy.

Right: The telegraph was among the many relatively recent technological developments that distinguished the Civil War from previous wars. This message from Colonel Robert Anderson, commander of Fort Sumter, describes in vivid language the Union efforts to hold the fort against the odds.

Opposite: The Gosport Naval Yard in Norfolk, Va, as it appeared in 1864. On April 20, 1861, having received word that Virginia militia were planning to seize the yard, post commander Charles S. McCauley gave orders to burn the facility then abandon it. But much of the machinery and artillery at Gosport remained in good condition when the Virginians arrived.

S.S.BALTIC.OFF SANDY HOOK APR.EIGHTEENTH.TEN THIRTY A.M. .VIA NEW YORK. . HON.S.CAMERON. SECY.WAR. WASHN. HAVING DEFENDED FORT SUMTER FOR THIRTY FOUR HOURS, UNTIL THE QUARTERS WERE ENTIRELY BURNED THE MAIN GATES DESTROYED BY FIRE.THE GORGE WALLS SERIOUSLY INJURED.THE MAGAZINE SURROUNDED BY FLAMES AND ITS DOOR CLOSED FROM THE EFFECTS OF HEAT .FOUR BARRELLS AND THREE CARTRIDGES OF POWDER ONLY BEING AVAILABLE AND NO PROVISIONS REMAINING BUT PORK.I ACCEPTED TERMS OF EVACUATION OFFERED BY GENERAL BEAUREGARD BEING ON SAME OFFERED BY HIM ON THE ELEVENTH INST.PRIOR TO THE COMMENCEMENT OF HOSTILITIES AND MARCHED OUT OF THE FORT SUNDAY AFTERNOON THE FOURTEENTH INST.WITH COLORS FLYING AND DRUMS BEATING.BRINGING AWAY COMPANY AND PRIVATE PROPERTY AND SALUTING MY FLAG WITH FIFTY GUNS. ROBERT ANDERSON.MAJOR FIRST ARTILLERY.COMMANDING.

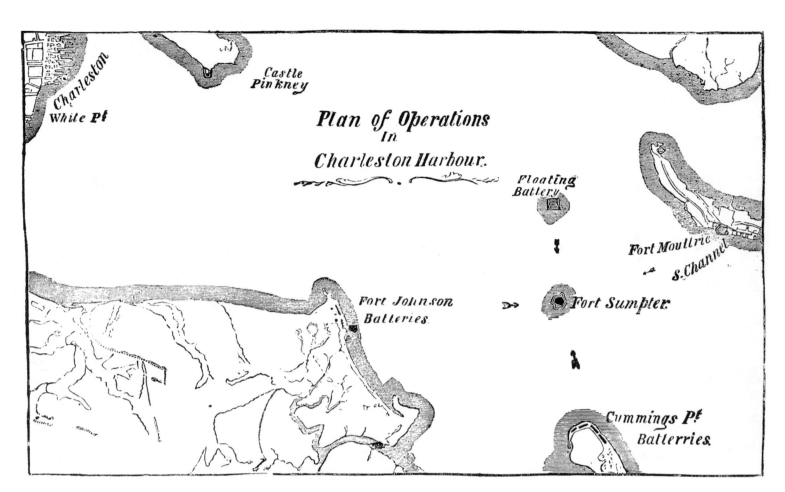

Plan of Operations
In
Charleston Harbour.

Right: Union sailors and commander McCauley flee Norfolk after setting fire to the six ships there. One of the ships that was burned to the waterline was the USS *Merrimack*. Shortly after capturing the yard, the Confederates began rebuilding the *Merrimack* as an ironclad. (They renamed it the CSS *Virginia*, but today it is generally referred to by its original name.)

Above: The April 27 issue of *Frank Leslie's Illustrated Newspaper* reports a "rumor" that the entrance to Norfolk harbor "has been blocked up by the sinking of small boats in the channel." "So far," the paper stated, "much confidence is expressed in the fidelity of the officer in command at the Yard, and also in his ability to defend it until assistance can be sent to him."

Opposite, bottom: Under the supervision of officers, slaves mount a cannon in preparation for the attack on Fort Sumter.

Opposite, top: A map of Charleston harbor showing points of attack on Fort Sumter (here misspelled).

Opposite: Residents of Charleston watch the bombardment of Fort Sumter from their roof-tops. This illustration appeared in the May 4 issue of *Harper's Weekly*. "The war has now begun in earnest," the paper announced. "Southerners have rebelled and dragged our flag in the dirt, in the belief that, because we won't fight duels or engage in street brawls, therefore we are cowards. The question now is whether or not they are right." The paper predicted that if Northerners were willing to fight and Lincoln was "up to his job," the war would be over by January 1862.

Right: Colonel Robert Anderson, commander of Fort Sumter. Anderson, a native of Kentucky, had been sent to Charleston in part because he was a Southerner; it was felt that a Northern officer's presence in the area would unnecessarily aggravate the growing tension. Although Anderson was unable successfully to defend Sumter, no one doubted that he made an heroic effort to do so. A month after the surrender he was promoted to the rank of brig. general.

Above: Federal troops spike the artillery at Fort Moultrie, S.C., before evacuating and moving to Sumter. About 80 US soldiers were stationed in the Charleston area when South Carolina seceded. Most of them were stationed at Moultrie, an older fort, located about a mile from Sumter. Anderson had warned Washington that Moultrie was especially vulnerable to land-based attack, and on December 11, nine days before South Carolina seceded, the War Department gave Anderson permission to transfer his command to Sumter if he deemed it necessary. On December 26, having already received demands for surrender, Anderson ordered Moultrie's guns spiked and the garrison transferred.

Right: Confederate General Pierre Gustave Toutant Beauregard, who had taken command at Charleston on March 1 under orders from Jefferson Davis. On April 12, at 4:30 a.m., his demands for immediate surrender having been refused by Anderson, Beauregard ordered Confederate artillery to open fire.

Opposite: Union troops fire Fort Sumter's cannons during the Southern bombardment.

Below: The exterior of Sumter after the Union surrender of the fort to General Beauregard.

"AN ARM'D RACE IS ADVANCING"

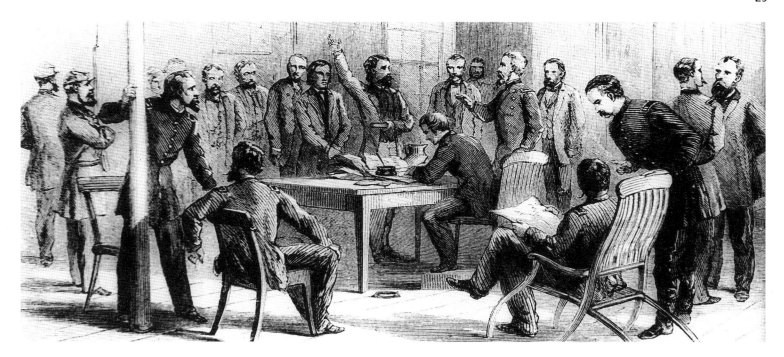

Above: A Southern volunteer takes an oath of allegiance to the Confederacy.

Below: A Confederate cartoon satirizes the North and its ''worship'' of blacks. Propaganda played an important role in reinforcing Southerners' contempt for Northerners and vice versa.

Opposite: Walt Whitman as he appeared in 1855 upon the publication of the first edition of *Leaves of Grass*. Whitman later wrote extensively about the war, capturing the mixture of excitement and sadness in New York City after the fall of Sumter:

The blood of the city up—arm'd! arm'd! the cry everywhere,
The flags flung out from the steeples of churches and from all the public buildings and stores,
The tearful parting, the mother kisses son . . .

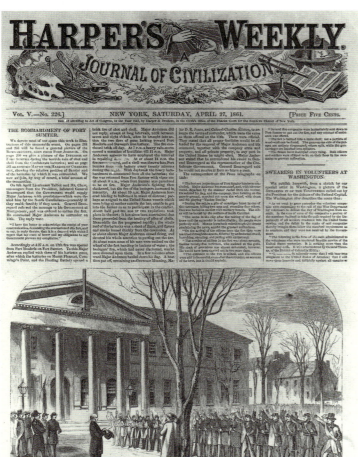

Above, left: General William Tecumseh Sherman, who was graduated from West Point in 1840 and later accepted a job as head of the Louisiana Academy. When South Carolina seceded Sherman left the deep South with mixed feelings: he had developed a fondness for the region and blamed politicians in Washington for allowing the confict to get out of hand.

Left: Northern volunteers take their oaths in Washington, shortly after the fall of Sumter. The day after the surrender of the fort Lincoln called 75,000 state militia into action for 90 days, primarily to protect Washington. Two days later, Virginia seceded. In a letter to Lincoln dated April 19 a Union loyalist in Virginia wrote that "Union feeling has been almost entirely swept out of existence." Within the next six weeks, Arkansas, North Carolina and Tennessee also joined the Confederacy.

Above: Robert E. Lee as he appeared at West Point. Lee had been opposed to secession and had mixed feelings about slavery. On April 18 Lincoln offered Lee command of Union armies. Lee refused, saying that loyalty to his state came first. Two days later he resigned his commission.

Opposite, top and bottom: Confederate sympathizers in Baltimore attack members of the 6th Massachusetts Regiment, who are on their way to Washington. Four soldiers and 12 civilians were killed in the clash, which occurred April 19. The regiment had been sent to protect the Capital. Most of the soldiers arrived safely.

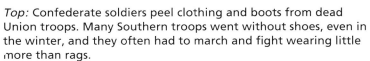

Top: Confederate soldiers peel clothing and boots from dead Union troops. Many Southern troops went without shoes, even in the winter, and they often had to march and fight wearing little more than rags.

Opposite: Union and Confederate soldiers swap newspapers and other items on the perimeters of their respective encampments. A Southern private recalled ''our boys and the Yanks'' picking berries together after striking a bargain not to fire at each other. We talked ''peacefully and kindly,'' he wrote, ''as if [we] had not been engaged for the last seven days in butchering each other.''

Above: A Union soldier watches for enemy movement from the attic of a private house.

Right: In this moving sketch Charles W. Reed depicts a soldier at the moment of a bullet's impact.

Right: Soldiers of the 4th New York Artillery load a cannon. In July, Congress authorized Lincoln to raise half a million volunteers. Ultimately, 700,000 men enlisted in the first year. By the end of the war, some 2.1 million men had fought for the Union, and 800,000 for the Confederacy.

Opposite: Union soldiers guard artillery in Virginia. Because of its overall industrial superiority the North had a decided advantage in artillery from the start of the war. In the foreground are mortars and mortar shells. Mortars were especially useful in seacoast defense because their plunging fire could inflict heavy damage on the decks of ships.

Above: Union General Gouverneur K. Warren, who would play a key role in the defense of Little Roundtop at Gettysburg, fortifies his lines. At the outset of the war, strong high-level leadership was not readily at hand. Many of the officers who would later become famous, including Grant, Sherman, Jackson and other West Point graduates, had resigned from the military after the War with Mexico. Meanwhile, 74-year-old General-in-Chief Winfield Scott and other high-ranking serving officers were showing signs of age.

Opposite, left: Noncommissioned officers of the 93rd New York Infantry relax over dinner. The Union soldier's diet generally consisted of beans, bacon, pickled beef, compressed mixed vegetables, and hardtack, the name for square biscuits made of flour and water.

Opposite, right: The Comte de Paris and officers play dominos at camp Winfield Scott in Yorktown, Va.

Below: Troops of the 1st Connecticut Artillery load 24-pound garrison guns at Fort Richardson, Va., in 1861. The Union raised 78 artillery regiments during the course of the war. The basic unit of field artillery was the battery, which comprised four to six cannons and about 100 men.

Right: A Union soldier prepares to fire a 10-pounder Parrot gun during a drill.

Above: A Union volunteer cavalryman. The Union cavalry was at first inferior to that of the Confederacy due to the fact that horsemanship was a highly valued skill in the antebellum South. Southerners liked to fancy themselves descendants of English cavaliers and Norman knights, and horses were a key aspect of this image. But horsemanship also had its practical side: the lack of paved roads in the South made travel on horseback much easier than travel by horse-drawn carriage and wagons. Years later, General Sherman said the South had had "the best cavalry in the world."

Top, left: Four artillery officers pose for the camera at Fair Oaks, Va.

Bottom, left: Soldiers in the Army of the Potomac fill a water cart. On July 27, 1861, Lincoln appointed Gen. George B. McClellan to command the Army of the Potomac. He replaced Irvin McDowell, who had been defeated at first Bull Run.

Opposite: Union troops converse at the Georgetown Ferry, across from 34th Street in Washington. Within two weeks after the fall of Sumter, 10,000 troops were stationed in the capital.

Left: Soldiers of the 3rd Georgia Infantry with their muskets. In 1861 many men of the North and South carried old-fashioned smooth-bore muskets. That same year, however, the Springfield Armory began manufacturing new rifled muskets which had a maximum range four times that of the old weapon. Over the next two years the armory turned out more than a quarter million new muskets.

Below: Confederate artillery men relax in camp after eating dinner. A lack of food seriously hampered the Confederate Army. The Southern soldiers often ate a mixture of cornmeal and bacon grease and felt lucky to get an occasional handful of black-eyed peas. As a result of poor diet, many men suffered from scurvy.

Opposite, top: Residents of Savannah, Georgia, turn out to cheer Confederate troops on their way to Virginia in August 1861. The Confederate Congress had authorized 500,000 volunteers by May.

Opposite, bottom left: A Union volunteer.

Opposite, bottom right: Private George W. Crane, of the 26th Illinois Infantry.

Opposite, top right: This drawing by Winslow Homer, who made numerous sketches of the war, shows the Zouave uniform, based on uniforms worn by the French in Algeria. Since states and towns provided uniforms early in the war, there was no consistency on either side. But by 1862 the blue uniform that we now associate with the Union had become official.

Opposite, top left: In another drawing by Homer, a Union soldier is shown loading his musket.

Opposite, bottom left: A fully outfitted private in the Union Infantry poses in front of a backdrop.

Opposite, bottom right: A volunteer tailors a Confederate soldier's uniform. The Confederate Army adopted gray as the official color but, due to short supply, was never able to maintain consistency in military dress.

Above: Union troops, under enemy fire, fall into formation. Early in the war, discipline was seriously lacking. One reason was a simple lack of prior military experience on the part of many soldiers. An additional problem was that armies on both sides allowed the soldiers themselves to elect lower and mid-level officers. As a result of this system, officers were sometimes reluctant to enforce discipline for fear of becoming unpopular with the troops.

Right: Charles R. Langdale in Union Zouave uniform, late in the war. The flashy uniform was a favorite among illustrators.

Top: An on-the-scene sketch by Winslow Homer shows Union infantry columns on the march. Marching discipline was particularly difficult to enforce early in the war. Shortly before the first Battle of Bull Run, for example, Union soldiers randomly fell out of line to pick blueberries and take naps.

Above: Soldiers of Company F, 114th Pennsylvania Infantry, in Petersburg, Va., during the summer of 1864.

Opposite, top right: A Union corporal in the Cavalry with saber and Spencer carbine. The saber had become largely a ceremonial weapon by the time of the Civil War.

Opposite, bottom: A Union recruiting station. As the drawing indicates, some towns began offering bounties to volunteers after initial enthusiasm for fighting had died down. The Union did not have to resort to a draft until 1863.

Opposite, top: Confederate volunteers march through the streets of Woodstock, Va., during a recruiting rally. On the strength of initial enthusiasm for defending Southern honor the Confederacy made it through the first year of the war without a draft. But slumping morale and a pool of potential soldiers that was only a third the size of the Union's forced the South to pass a conscription law in the spring of 1862.

Opposite, bottom: Union troops shoulder their muskets and prepare to march towards Harper's Ferry, Va.

Right: Cover of sheet music for the Confederate anthem, ''God Save the South.'' Music played an important role in boosting morale. The power of music during the war was recognized by Union General Benjamin F. Butler among others: as military governor of New Orleans, Butler arrested the publisher of a popular song titled ''Bonnie Blue Flag'' and announced that anyone heard singing it would be fined.

Below: Hardtack and eating utensils from a Union soldier's pack. Soldiers often joked that hardtack was so hard it could stop bullets.

Above: A Union regiment waits for marching orders.

Left: Winslow Homer drawing of soldiers on the march. Homer covered the Army of the Potomac in the spring of 1862 for *Harper's Weekly*, and later followed Grant's troops in the Wilderness. Although many of his published illustrations were of battle scenes, Homer preferred to sketch soldiers at ease because that was when their personalities came through. Several of these sketches he later worked up into full-fledged paintings, and some of these – *The Briarwood Pipe*, for example, or *Prisoners from the Front* – are now among his best-known works.

Opposite: A soldier dries his laundry on the end of his musket.

Below: A gun crew races into battle. Typically, when the crew reached its firing position, the gun would be unlocked and maneuvered to face the enemy; the surplus ammunition, meanwhile, would be taken to the rear so as to avoid an accidental explosion.

Opposite, top: A confederate deserter crosses the Union line. Desertions from the Confederacy, rare in the first year of the war, increased in 1862, in part because the faltering Southern economy was taking its toll back home. "Poor men have been compelled to leave the army to come home to provide for their families," wrote one Mississippi soldier in December 1861. ". . . we are willing to defend our country but our families [come] first." By 1865, desertion, as one Confederate officer put it, had become an "epidemic" due to plummeting morale as well as a failing economy.

Left: Portrait of a Union soldier. Desertion was a problem for the North as well: One historian has estimated that there were 200,000 desertions from the Union. About 150 deserters were executed. In all, the South lost about 13 percent of its army to deserters; the North, roughly nine percent.

Left: A recruiting poster for the 12th Massachusetts Battery, under the command of General Nathaniel P. Banks. Banks was one of a number of political generals appointed to the Union Army for their ability to attract support for the war. He replaced Robert Patterson, a 69-year-old general after the Union loss at first Bull Run.

Below: First Connecticut heavy artillery at Fort Richardson.

Opposite, top: Various Confederate uniforms. Many of these costumes were worn more for parade than for campaigning and, at that, were probably used only in the early years of the war.

Opposite, bottom: Women volunteers hard at work sewing uniforms.

UNIFORMS OF THE CONFEDERATE ARMY.

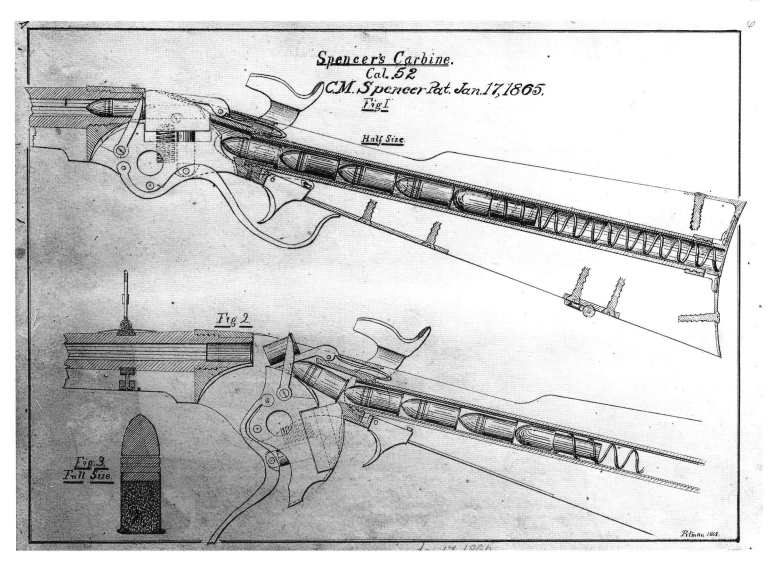

Spencer's Carbine.
Cal. 52
C.M. Spencer Pat. Jan. 17, 1865.
Fig. 1

Half Size.

Fig. 2

Fig. 3
Full Size.

Pitman 1868.

Opposite, top: Union soldiers with a 13-inch mortar, which weighed 20,000 pounds and fired shells weighing 220 pounds. Generally they were mounted on railroad cars. In this case, a stationary platform was used.

Opposite, bottom: An illustration from a November 1860 issue of *Harper's Weekly,* titled "Training Day in the Country," called attention to the lack of discipline among recruits.

Above: A cross-section of the Spencer carbine, the first lever-action repeater. One Rebel is supposed to have referred to the Spencer as "that tarnation Yankee gun they loads on Sunday and shoots the rest of the week."

Right: A "Coffee Mill" machine gun, which, with its hand crank and feed hopper, resembled the coffee grinders of the period. It took two men to fire the gun: one to load cartridges into the hopper and one to aim and turn the crank. Having initially rejected it, the Union later paid $850 apiece. By comparison, the 10-pounder cannon cost a little over $200.

BLOCKADE

Right: Warships patrol the coast just outside Charleston harbor. Under the leadership of Secretary Gideon Welles and Assistant Secretary Gustavus V. Fox the Union Navy rapidly built an impressive fleet and gained naval superiority over the Confederacy. At the end of 1861 the Union had 42 warships; by the end of the war it had nearly 700 vessels of various kinds. Ultimately, superiority at sea was a key to the Union's victory.

Above: The frigate USS *St. Lawrence* sinks the *Petrel*, a Rebel privateer. On April 17 Jefferson Davis announced he would officially sanction private ships that wished to attack Union vessels and seize their cargo. Lincoln considered privateer crews to be nothing more than pirates and initially threatened to hang any who were captured. Later, however, to protect Union prisoners of war from a similar fate, he backed away from his threat and ordered that captured privateer crews be treated simply as prisoners of war.

Opposite: The USS *San Jacinto* stops the British packet *Trent*. On April 19 Lincoln ordered a blockade of all major Southern ports. The blockade severely hampered the Confederate economy and war effort. But it also had international political implications, and almost backfired on the Union during the *Trent* affair.

Opposite, top: The *Colonel Lamb*, a Confederate blockade-runner built in Liverpool. The South's dependence on European goods and Europe's need for Southern cotton meant that England had an interest in aiding the blockade-running effort. A number of steamers were built in England specifically for this purpose.

Opposite, bottom: A Union ship pursues a blockade runner. The Union failed to capture most blockade runners during the first year of the war, but the rate of interception grew steadily thereafter, rising to nearly 50 percent in 1865. The cumulative effect of the blockade on the South's already-weak economy was devastating.

Above: Captured British blockade runners lie at anchor in New York Harbor.

Right: A Union recruiting poster for the Virginia Coast Guard. In total, about 100,000 men served in the Union Navy.

RECRUITS WANTED!

WANTED IMMEDIATELY,

250 SAILORS

TO RECRUIT FOR THE

VIRGINIA COAST GUARD.

NOW STATIONED AT

FORTRESS MONROE.

They are to be inspected and enlisted in New-York, by order of Major General Butler, by Captain T. Bailey Myers, an Officer of his Staff, on special duty in New-York. None but those at least five feet four inches in height, and able bodied, need apply.

PAY TO DATE FROM DAY OF MUSTERING IN.

RENDEVOUS, 360 PEARL-STREET;

OPEN FROM 10 A.M. TO 3 P.M.

D. H. BURTNETT,
Major Va. C. G. Recruiting Office.

I am authorized to inspect and enlist the above recruits, by an order from Major General Butler, dated Fortress Monroe, June 16th, 1861.

T. BAILEY MYERS,
Captain, and Acting A. Q. M.

Portsmouth.

Gun boat Fanny

from a sketch by Lieu Le

Destruction of Fort Ocracoke on Beacon island entrance to Pamplico sound
expedition under command of Lieut Eastman of the Pawnee. Sept. 17th.

Opposite, top: Union warships *Cumberland* and *Saratoga* engage the Confederate steamer *Jamestown* off Newport News, Va., near Norfolk. This drawing appeared in the *New York Illustrated News* in September, 1861.

Opposite, bottom: A Union expedition ship destroys Fort Ocracoke on Beacon Island, near Cape Hatteras, North Carolina, in September, 1861. Two months earlier Navy officials had realized that they must seize key harbors along the Southern coast if they were to maintain an effective blockade. On August 27 an expedition under the command of Benjamin Butler took two forts at Hatteras Inlet. A string of similar expeditions followed, including a successful attack on Port Royal, South Carolina, one of the finest and best defended harbors in the South.

Above: A British-built blockade runner, the *Lord Clyde*. The low, sleek design, typical of blockade runners, made the ship fast and hard to intercept, though this particular vessel was later captured by the Union. It remained in active service in the US Navy until 1883.

Right: Captain Raphael Semmes, foreground, and Lt. J.M. Kell, aboard the *Alabama*, the most successful of all the British-built Southern commerce raiders. The *Alabama* destroyed more than 60 merchant ships before going down off the coast of France in a battle with the Union sloop-of-war USS *Kearsarge*.

THE ROAD TO BULL RUN

Opposite: Union and Confederate troops clash in the first Battle of Bull Run. On May 21 the Confederate Congress decided to move its capital from Montgomery to Richmond, thus setting the stage for the war's first major battle. General Beauregard deployed 20,000 troops on the south bank of Bull Run, with 12,000 more 50 miles northwest in the Shenandoah Valley. On July 16, 35,000 Union troops under General Irvin McDowell began to advance from the Potomac to Beauregard's defenses at Manassas.

Right: General Thomas "Stonewall" Jackson at the Battle of Bull Run. On the morning of July 21, the battle began in earnest, and by noon Confederate forces had been driven back from their original position to Henry House Hill. When South Carolina troops under General Barnard Bee began to falter, Bee yelled out, "There is Jackson standing behind you like a stone wall! Rally behind the Virginians!" Bee was killed shortly thereafter, but his men did rally behind Jackson's troops.

Above: The Rhode Island brigade of Colonel Ambrose E. Burnside and the 71st New York approaching Manassas on July 18, 1861.

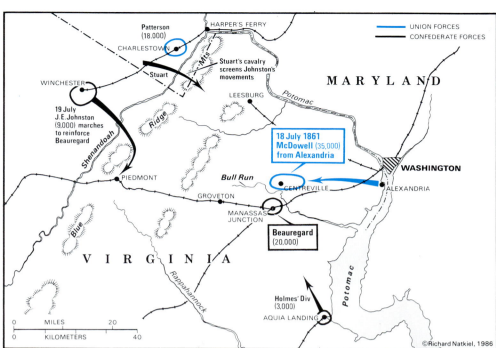

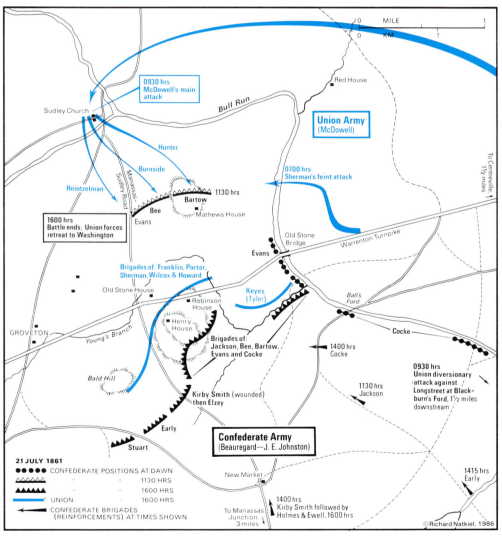

Above: Colonel Burnside's brigade. As the Union Army began its retreat, most Confederates were too tired or disorganized to follow. A few, however, did follow in pursuit. Burnside later recalled that the enemy continued to "play [its] artillery upon the carriages, ambulances, and artillery wagons. . . . Several persons were killed or dangerously wounded."

Opposite: The stone house near Bull Run where the Confederates wavered before being pushed back to Henry Hill. After losing this position, General Bee announced that "all was lost" unless he could get reinforcements. Those reinforcements did arrive under the command of General Joseph Johnston, who had eluded Patterson in the valley. The fresh troops gave the Confederates the final advantage, and by dusk the battle was virtually over. The Confederates had won a major victory.

Right: Maps show the first Battle of Bull Run. The map on top shows the approach to battle. The map on bottom shows the position of Union and Confederate lines on July 21. The Union and Confederate armies lost about 600 men each in the battle – a small number of casualties compared with the battles to come.

Top: A cartoon shows the key players in the *Trent* affair: (l to r) Britain's Earl Russell, Confederate envoys to England Mason and Slidell, Secretary of State Seward, and Jefferson Davis.

Opposite, above and right: Northern cartoons decry British trade with the South but imply that Union trade with Britain is simply humanitarian.

Above: Union sailors apprehend Mason and Sliddell aboard the *Trent*. On November 8, 1861, the USS *San Jacinto* stopped the *Trent*, a British mail vessel, having learned that Mason and Slidell were aboard. The *San Jacinto*'s captain, Charles Wilkes, subsequently arrested the two men and sent them to a prison in Boston. When word of the incident reached England, British politicians and the British public were furious. For a brief period, it appeard that England might enter the war against the Union. Lincoln resolved the crisis by releasing Mason and Slidell and saved face by implying that Wilkes had acted without authority.

Opposite, top: Union and Confederate soldiers clash near Fall's Church, Va. Although no major battles occurred for the remainder of 1861, there were many such skirmishes in the aftermath of first Bull Run.

Opposite, bottom left: A Currier & Ives lithograph depicts a soldier leaving his family. The Battle of Bull Run forced upon the North *and* the South the realization that the war would not end as soon as had been anticipated.

Opposite, bottom right: The cover of sheet music to "Hail! Glorious Banner," one of countless patriotic songs composed during the Civil War. The dedication to General George McClellan reflects the initial enthusiasm surrounding McClellan's appointment as commander of the Army of Potomac after the defeat at Bull Run. Charles Coffin, a newspaper reporter, wrote that people were beginning to call him "the Young Napoleon."

Left: Soldiers of the first Rhode Island Regiment bed down in the Patent Office in Washington which also served as a hospital. Walt Whitman wrote, "It was a strange, solemn . . . [but] sort of fascinating sight," he wrote. Amidst glass cases "crowded with models in miniature of every kind of utensil, machine or invention" lay rows of sick and wounded, many of whom were amputees.

Opposite, left: Soldiers of the 71st New York Volunteer Infantry prepare dinner. After Bull Run, volunteers poured into the capital. Coffin reported that "In every village drums were beating, soldiers marching." By October, McClellan had 120,000 men under his command.

Opposite, right: Confederate soldiers make camp at the Warrington Navy Yard in Pensacola, Florida.

Below: The 5th Vermont at Camp Griffin, Va., in 1861.

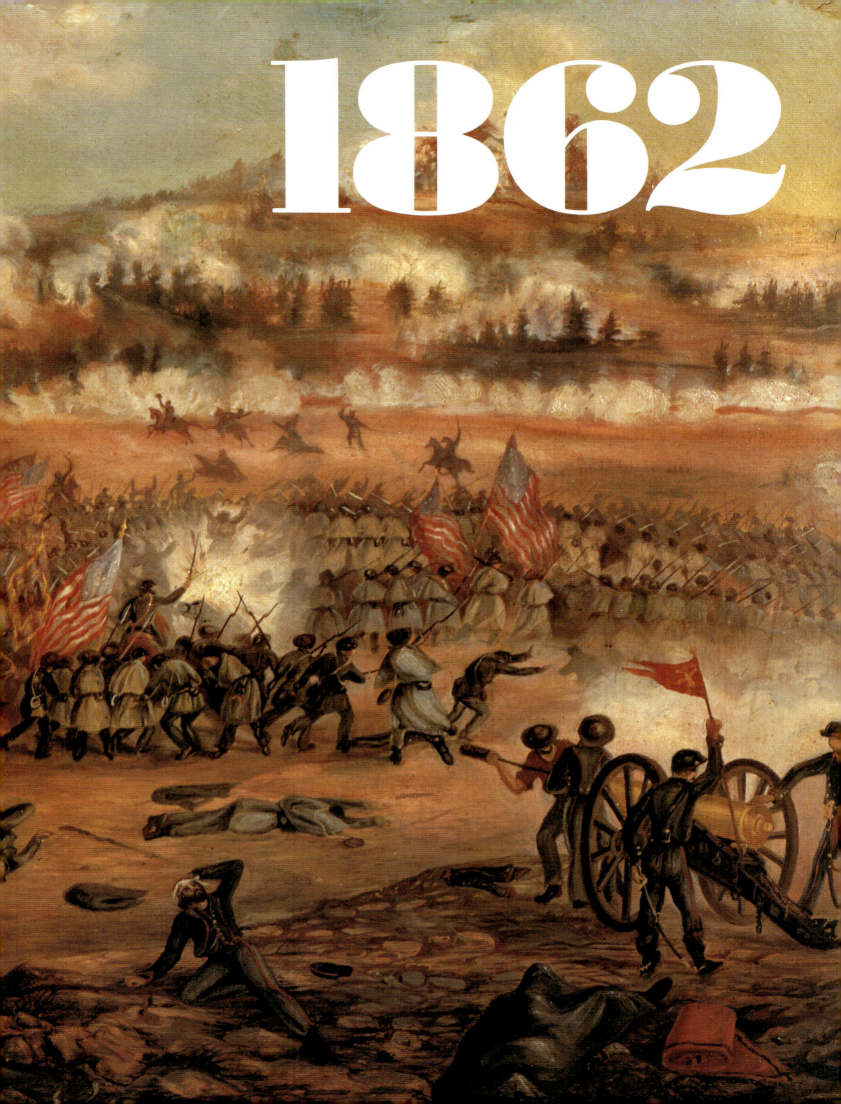

1862

"No terms except for immediate and unconditional surrender can be accepted."

Ulysses S. Grant, February 1862

The Confederate victory at Bull Run and the humiliation of the Trent Affair (in which an angry Great Britain had forced the North to release two Southerners who had been taken prisoner while sailing as passengers on a British ship) had severely undermined Union morale in 1861. McClellan's appointment briefly lifted Northern spirits, but by January 1862 he was still preparing his army for battle, and Northerners were growing increasingly impatient at his inaction.

What these discouraged Yankees failed to realize as the New Year unfolded was that they had on their side another leader who possessed all the qualities McClellan lacked. Ulysses S. Grant was still relatively unknown, and it would be another 18 months before he would emerge as the Union's most talented battlefield commander. But in early February he gave the Union its sorely-needed first victory.

While McClellan was still formulating grandiose plans for his offensive against Richmond via the Virginia peninsula, Grant was closing in on Fort Henry, a strategically important installation on the Tennessee River. By February 6 Union gunboats had captured the fort, and Grant had turned his attention to Fort Donelson, 12 miles away. The second battle proved to be more difficult than the first, but during the assault Grant demonstrated one of his most important attributes – coolness under fire – and managed to rally his troops to victory. His subsequent refusal to negotiate terms of surrender earned him the nickname "Unconditional Surrender" Grant and gave the North a new feeling of hope.

The following month, Lincoln relieved McClellan of his position as general in chief, arguing that he could not serve in this capacity while commanding troops in the field. At the same time, he reluctantly approved McClellan's proposal to ferry the army down the Potomac and the Chesapeake Bay and attack Richmond from the southeast. By April, McClellan had nearly 100,000 men on the Virginia peninsula between the York and James rivers. The Rebel Army was less than half that size, but over the next three months the "Young Napoleon" would repeatedly fail to press his advantage. The campaign culminated in a week-long series of battles near Richmond in which the Confederates, now under Robert E. Lee, suffered nearly 20,000 casualties but nonetheless managed to repulse the Union forces. One Union commander, outraged by McClellan's order to retreat, suggested that the general was guilty of either "cowardice or treason."

In spite of his disappointment, Lincoln did not remove McClellan from command, and in September, McClellan was given an extraordinary opportunity to redeem himself. Early that month Lee's army had invaded Maryland. As McClellan was preparing to meet the Rebel forces, he stumbled upon a copy of Lee's battle orders in an abandoned camp. Now he not only had a decided numerical advantage, he had precise knowledge of Rebel movements. Had he acted quickly, he might well have been able to destroy Lee's army. Instead, he hesitated for 16 hours. Lee, meanwhile, took the extra time to reposition his forces.

On September 17 the two armies finally clashed near Antietam Creek outside the town of Sharpsburg. It turned out to

Previous pages: The Battle of Fredericksburg.

Left: An Alfred Waud sketch of the Battle of Kernstown, fought near Winchester, Va., on March 23, 1862. It marked the opening of Stonewall Jackson's brilliant Shenandoah Valley campaign.

Opposite: An artist's version of Abraham Lincoln composing the Emancipation Proclamation.

be the bloodiest day of the war, but when it was over neither side had won a decisive victory. The political significance of the battle, on the other hand, turned out to be enormous.

Two months earlier, Lincoln had drawn up his Emancipation Proclamation but had delayed announcing it until the North had won a military victory. In spite of McClellan's poor performance, the Federals had at least repulsed the Rebels from Maryland, and politically that was all the President needed. On September 22 Lincoln announced the proclamation, which was to take effect the following January. The announcement dramatically changed the focus of the war.

Preservation of the Union was still paramount, but the abolition of slavery was now propelling the North's war effort.

Having changed his political strategy, Lincoln turned back to problems of military leadership. On November 5 he removed McClellan from command and appointed Ambrose Burnside to head the Army of the Potomac. The following month, the new commander led his army into battle at Fredericksburg and suffered one of the most devastating defeats of the war. The North was once again consumed by despair, and it would be another six months before a pair of major victories would turn the tide in the Union's favor.

THE WAR IN THE WEST

Opposite: Union soldiers under the command of Ulysses S. Grant attack Fort Donelson, one of two strategically important Tennessee forts located just south of the Kentucky border near the Cumberland and Tennessee rivers; the other was Fort Henry. Grant had occupied northern Kentucky since the fall of 1861. On February 6, 1862, his force of 15,000 men attacked Fort Henry by land while Union gunboats fired on the fort from the Tennessee River.

Above: Another view of the battle of Fort Donelson. On February 13, now backed by an army of 27,000 men, Grant attacked Donelson. Confederates managed to push the Union infantry back while damaging three Union gunboats. The Rebels followed up with an attack that opened an escape route but hesitated and returned to their trenches. Confederate command was passed from Gen. Floyd to Gen. Pillow to Gen. Buckner, who was forced to agree to Grant's terms of ''unconditional and immediate'' surrender.

Right: The capture of Fort Donelson. Grant's success in this expedition was important not only for strategic reasons but because it helped boost morale in the North.

Opposite, top: Union gunboats under the command of Flag Officer Andrew Foote (lower half of picture) fire on Fort Donelson from the Tennessee River. The upper half of the picture shows Confederate batteries during the attack.

Opposite, bottom: The Battle of Shiloh, or Pittsburgh Landing, Tennessee, begins. Grant had established a base at Pittsburgh Landing in March and was subsequently reinforced by several divisions. Confederate General Albert Sidney Johnston, marched his troops to Pittsburgh Landing from Corinth, Mississippi, and on the morning of April 6, 1862, ordered the assault. After Johnston was killed, the Confederates advanced under Beauregard, but did not win .

Right: Confederate officers huddle as the Battle of Shiloh begins.

Below: The 14th Wisconsin Regiment, foreground, charges into Confederate artillery fire on the second day of fighting at Shiloh.

Shiloh: the first day

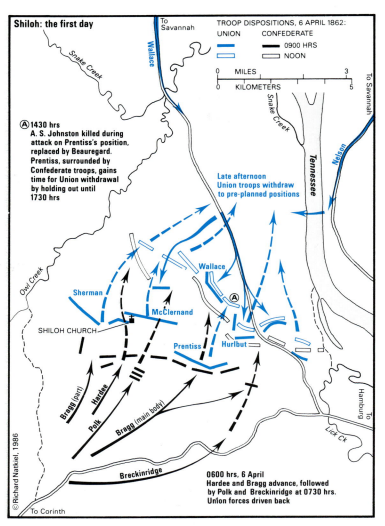

TROOP DISPOSITIONS, 6 APRIL 1862:
UNION   CONFEDERATE
0900 HRS
NOON

To Savannah
Wallace
Snake Creek
Tennessee
Nelson

Ⓐ 1430 hrs
A. S. Johnston killed during attack on Prentiss's position, replaced by Beauregard. Prentiss, surrounded by Confederate troops, gains time for Union withdrawal by holding out until 1730 hrs

Late afternoon Union troops withdraw to pre-planned positions

Wallace
Sherman
McClernand
SHILOH CHURCH
Prentiss
Hurlbut
Ⓐ

Owl Creek
Bragg (part)
Polk
Hardee
Bragg (main body)
Breckinridge

To Hamburg
Lick Ck

0600 hrs, 6 April
Hardee and Bragg advance, followed by Polk and Breckinridge at 0730 hrs. Union forces driven back

© Richard Natkiel, 1986
To Corinth

Shiloh: the second day

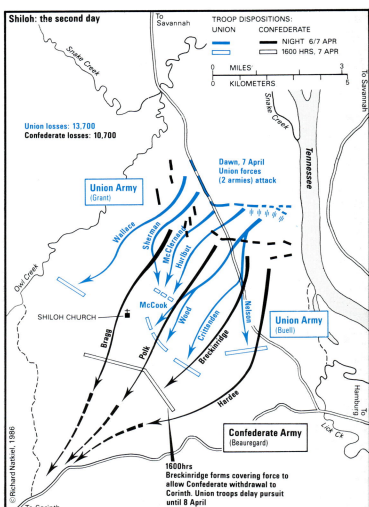

TROOP DISPOSITIONS:
UNION   CONFEDERATE
NIGHT 6/7 APR
1600 HRS, 7 APR

To Savannah
Snake Creek
Tennessee

Union losses: 13,700
Confederate losses: 10,700

Dawn, 7 April
Union forces (2 armies) attack

Union Army (Grant)

Wallace
Sherman
McClernand
Hurlbut
McCook
Wood
Crittenden
Nelson

SHILOH CHURCH
Bragg
Polk
Breckinridge
Hardee

Union Army (Buell)

Confederate Army (Beauregard)

Owl Creek
To Hamburg
Lick Ck

1600hrs
Breckinridge forms covering force to allow Confederate withdrawal to Corinth. Union troops delay pursuit until 8 April

© Richard Natkiel, 1986
To Corinth

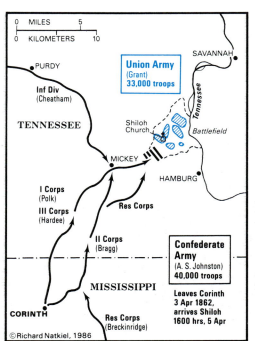

MILES 5
KILOMETERS 10

PURDY
Inf Div (Cheatham)
TENNESSEE

Union Army (Grant) 33,000 troops

SAVANNAH
Shiloh Church
Battlefield
Tennessee
MICKEY
HAMBURG

I Corps (Polk)
III Corps (Hardee)
Res Corps
II Corps (Bragg)

MISSISSIPPI

CORINTH
Res Corps (Breckinridge)

Confederate Army (A. S. Johnston) 40,000 troops

Leaves Corinth 3 Apr 1862, arrives Shiloh 1600 hrs, 5 Apr

© Richard Natkiel, 1986

THE ASSAULT ON FORT DO[...]

Top: The map on the left shows the battle lines on the first day of fighting at Shiloh; the map on the right shows positions on the second day. After nightfall on the first day a ferocious storm moved in, and streaks of lightning mingled with the flashes of guns to illuminate the nightmarish landscape. Jesse Young, a soldier in Sherman's division, recalled that he would ''catch every now and then an occasional cry of a maimed and mangled soldier . . . lying helpless and bleeding on the wet earth.''

Above, left: Johnston's approach from Corinth. The march of just 18 miles had taken three days due to inexperience and fatigue on the part of the Rebel soldiers.

Above: The assault on Fort Donelson.

Opposite, top and bottom: The Battle of Shiloh, an overview, and close-up.

THE IRONCLADS

Opposite: The USS *Monitor* (foreground) and the *Merrimack* (CSS *Virginia*) exchange fire. On March 8, 1862, the *Merrimack* attacked Union ships guarding Hampton Roads. Throughout the day it appeared that the Confederate ironclad might be invincible, but that night the Union's new ironclad, the *Monitor*, arrived on the scene, and the following morning the historic clash began.

Top: A bird's eye view of Hampton Roads during the battle of the ironclads.

Above, left: The dented turret of the *Monitor* after the battle. Ironclads at first proved almost impervious to gunfire. Only after the war were munitions developed that could penetrate their armor.

Above, right: John Ericsson, designer of the *Monitor*. Not all Northerners were impressed with this new armored warship. When Nathaniel Hawthorne saw it, he asked, ''How can an admiral condescend to go to sea in an iron pot? . . . All the pomp and splendor of naval warfare are gone by.'' He went on to predict that with this new development ''heroism'' would become a ''quality of minor importance, [since] its possessor cannot break through the iron crust of his own armament and give the world a glimpse of it.''

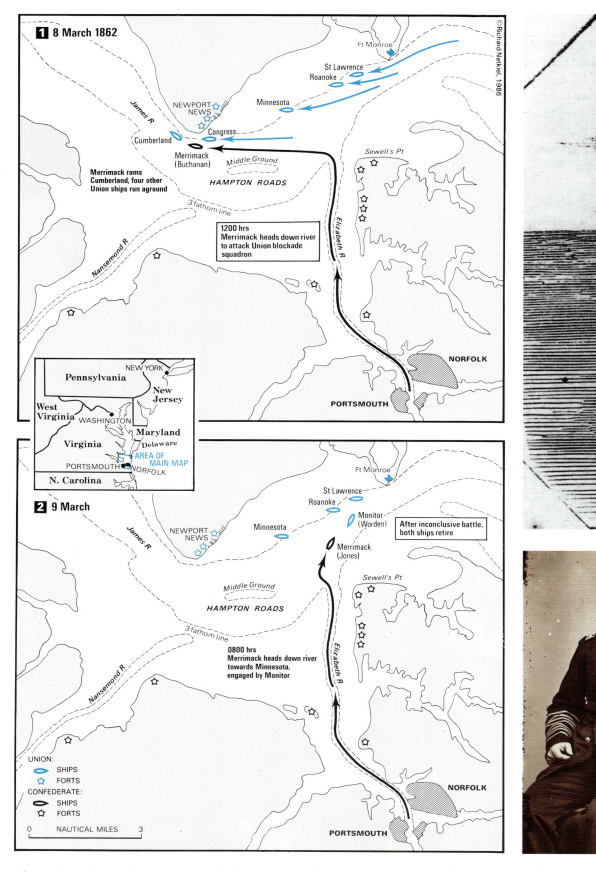

1 8 March 1862

Ft Monroe

St Lawrence
Roanoke

Minnesota

NEWPORT NEWS

Congress

Cumberland

Merrimack
(Buchanan)

Middle Ground

Merrimack rams Cumberland, four other Union ships run aground

James R

Nansemond R

3 fathom line

HAMPTON ROADS

1200 hrs Merrimack heads down river to attack Union blockade squadron

Sewell's Pt

Elizabeth R

NORFOLK

PORTSMOUTH

© Richard Natkiel, 1986

NEW YORK

Pennsylvania

New Jersey

West Virginia

WASHINGTON

Virginia

Maryland

Delaware

AREA OF MAIN MAP

PORTSMOUTH NORFOLK

N. Carolina

2 9 March

Ft Monroe

St Lawrence
Roanoke

Monitor
(Worden)

After inconclusive battle, both ships retire

NEWPORT NEWS

Minnesota

Merrimack
(Jones)

Sewell's Pt

James R

Middle Ground

HAMPTON ROADS

Nansemond R

3 fathom line

0800 hrs Merrimack heads down river towards Minnesota, engaged by Monitor

Elizabeth R

NORFOLK

PORTSMOUTH

UNION:
SHIPS
FORTS
CONFEDERATE:
SHIPS
FORTS

0   NAUTICAL MILES   3

Above: Maps shows the movement of the *Merrimack* (i.e., *Virginia*) before the *Monitor*'s arrival, top, and the location of the battle between the ironclads. The battle was inconclusive, but its historical significance – the end of the "Age of Fighting Sail" – was immense.

Above, lower right: Admiral David G. Farragut, who commanded a fleet of 17 wooden ships and sailed up the Mississippi River to New Orleans. On April 24 the forts south of the city, having

already withstood heavy Union mortar fire, opened fire on the old-fashioned fleet. Farragut lost only one ship and the next day New Orleans surrendered.

Opposite, top: The *Monitor*, which measured 172 feet from bow to stern.

Opposite, bottom: The frigate *Cumberland*, one of two Union ships destroyed by the *Merrimack* before the *Monitor*'s arrival.

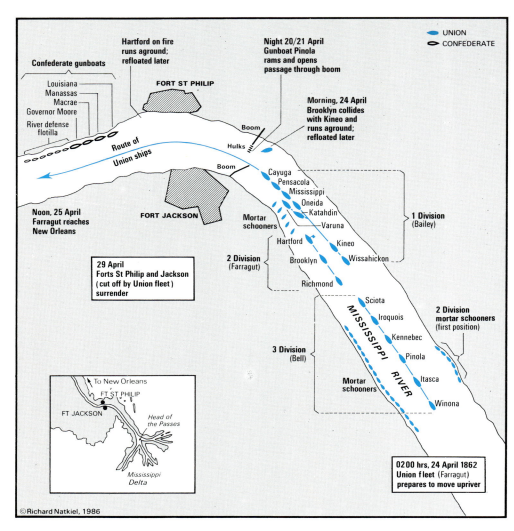

Top: Farragut's movement up the Mississippi River. After conquering New Orleans, the admiral continued up the river taking Baton Rouge and Natchez. He had hoped to take Vicksburg as well but failed and retreated.

Above: The *Merrimack*. Two months after the battle with the *Monitor* the Confederates destroyed the celebrated ironclad to prevent it from falling into enemy hands as the Union reclaimed Norfolk Naval Yard.

Right: Sailors wounded when the *Merrimack* destroyed a Union vessel are carried ashore as the Ironclads engage in battle.

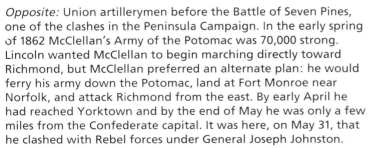

Opposite: Union artillerymen before the Battle of Seven Pines, one of the clashes in the Peninsula Campaign. In the early spring of 1862 McClellan's Army of the Potomac was 70,000 strong. Lincoln wanted McClellan to begin marching directly toward Richmond, but McClellan preferred an alternate plan: he would ferry his army down the Potomac, land at Fort Monroe near Norfolk, and attack Richmond from the east. By early April he had reached Yorktown and by the end of May he was only a few miles from the Confederate capital. It was here, on May 31, that he clashed with Rebel forces under General Joseph Johnston.

Top: The Battle of Seven Pines, also known as Fair Oaks. McClellan was at a disadvantage because his army was divided by the Chickahominy River. Johnston had planned to attack the smaller Union force at dawn but confusion over his orders delayed the offensive for several hours. This allowed McClellan time to consolidate. As a result, what might have been a rout

ended in a virtual draw – albeit at great cost. The Union lost 5000 men, the Rebels, over 6000. The most significant result of the battle was that Johnston was wounded and was replaced by Robert E. Lee.

Above, left: An 1862 sketch showing McClellan's Army landing in Hampton, Va.

Above, right: A Union battery manned by soldiers from the 7th Connecticut Regiment fires on the Confederates at Yorktown on May 4. A month earlier, when McClellan landed in Virginia, he had overestimated the size of the Rebel force at Yorktown and had settled in for a siege. Finally, in early May, he was ready to attack, but by this time it was too late to have any real impact, for on May 3, realizing the Confederates were severely outnumbered, Johnston had withdrawn his forces toward Richmond.

Battle of Winchester

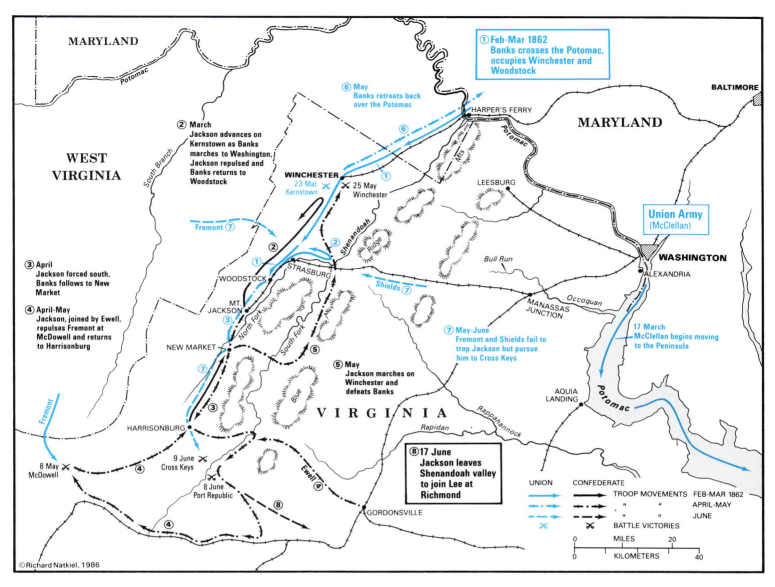

MARYLAND

WEST VIRGINIA

① Feb-Mar 1862
Banks crosses the Potomac, occupies Winchester and Woodstock

⑥ May
Banks retreats back over the Potomac

② March
Jackson advances on Kernstown as Banks marches to Washington, Jackson repulsed and Banks returns to Woodstock

③ April
Jackson forced south, Banks follows to New Market

④ April-May
Jackson, joined by Ewell, repulses Fremont at McDowell and returns to Harrisonburg

⑤ May
Jackson marches on Winchester and defeats Banks

⑦ May-June
Fremont and Shields fail to trap Jackson but pursue him to Cross Keys

⑧ 17 June
Jackson leaves Shenandoah valley to join Lee at Richmond

Union Army (McClellan)

17 March
McClellan begins moving to the Peninsula

VIRGINIA

WINCHESTER 23 Mar Kernstown 25 May Winchester

WOODSTOCK · STRASBURG · MT. JACKSON · NEW MARKET · HARRISONBURG

8 May McDowell · 9 June Cross Keys · 8 June Port Republic · GORDONSVILLE

BALTIMORE · HARPER'S FERRY · LEESBURG · WASHINGTON · ALEXANDRIA · MANASSAS JUNCTION · AQUIA LANDING

© Richard Natkiel, 1986

UNION CONFEDERATE
TROOP MOVEMENTS FEB-MAR 1862
APRIL-MAY
JUNE
BATTLE VICTORIES

MILES 20 / KILOMETERS 40

Opposite, top: A Winslow Homer sketch depicting a skirmish at Lee's Mills on April 16 during the siege at Yorktown.

Opposite, bottom: Union soldiers under Nathaniel Banks charge the stone wall at the Battle of Winchester on May 25. Part of Jackson's Valley Campaign, the battle ended in decisive victory for the Confederates.

Top: Jackson's Valley Campaign. In late April, Jackson had an army of 17,000 men in the Shenandoah Valley. The Union had nearly twice that number, under the command of Nathaniel Banks and John C. Frémont. Jackson prevented these Union forces from reinforcing McClellan by repeatedly defeating them.

Far right: General Thomas "Stonewall" Jackson. "He drove us like hell," one of his soldiers later recalled, but he pushed himself at least as hard as he pushed his men.

Right: Confederate General Jeb Stuart, arguably the best Confederate cavalry leader in the war.

Opposite, top: General Banks recrosses the Potomac from Williamsport, Md., on May 7, after having been defeated by Jackson at Winchester.

Opposite, bottom right and left: Union General John C. Frémont.

Top: The Battle of Williamsburg, May 4, was one of the fights that took place as McClellan clumsily pursued the Rebels after their withdrawal from Yorktown.

Left: General Robert E. Lee rides majestically into battle on his horse Traveler. Lee was graduated from West Point, second in his class, in 1829 and received a commission in the Engineer Corps. When the Mexican War broke out, he joined Winfield Scott's staff and was eventually promoted to colonel for the bravery and skill he displayed in the Mexico City campaign. During the first year of the Civil War he failed to distinguish himself, but in the spring of 1862 he became Davis's military advisor, and after Joseph Johnston was wounded he took command of the Army of Northern Virginia.

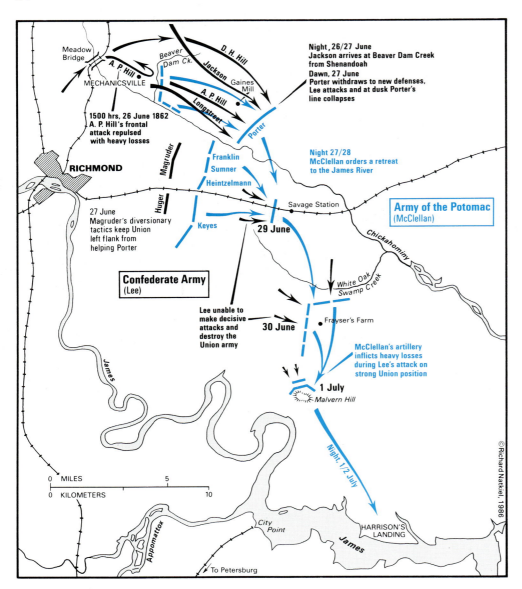

Night, 26/27 June
Jackson arrives at Beaver Dam Creek
from Shenandoah
Dawn, 27 June
Porter withdraws to new defenses,
Lee attacks and at dusk Porter's
line collapses

1500 hrs, 26 June 1862
A. P. Hill's frontal
attack repulsed
with heavy losses

Night 27/28 June
McClellan orders a retreat
to the James River

27 June
Magruder's diversionary
tactics keep Union left flank from
helping Porter

Army of the Potomac
(McClellan)

Confederate Army
(Lee)

Lee unable to
make decisive
attacks and
destroy the
Union army

McClellan's artillery
inflicts heavy losses
during Lee's attack on
strong Union position

©Richard Natkiel, 1986

Left: The Seven Days' Battles.

Below: An engraving from *Harper's Weekly* by John R. Chapin. The sketch was done as General McClellan's Army was landing at Hampton, Va.

Opposite, top and bottom: Union cavalrymen pursue Rebels after the evacuation of Yorktown. The sketch at bottom, by Alfred R. Waud, was done at the scene and appeared in *Harper's Weekly* a short time later.

Pursuit of the flying rebels

96

Left: General Philip Kearney's troops charge on May 5, 1862, during the Peninsula campaign.

Below: Inflation of the "Intrepid," a hot-air balloon used in reconnaissance in the battle of Fair Oaks.

Opposite, top: Confederates leave Mechanicsville as Union batteries shell the village on May 24.

Opposite, bottom: The march from Williamsburg during the Peninsula campaign.

Above: The frame house, used as a hospital during the Battle of Fair Oaks.

Top center: Bayonet charge of the New York Excelsior Brigade, Colonel Hall commanding, at the Battle of Fair Oaks on May 31.

Opposite, top right: The Government burial corps disinters the remains of Union soldiers killed at Fair Oaks.

Right: The Battle of Fair Oaks was in some respects the high point of McClellan's drive up the peninsula toward Richmond. The Union made few gains in the weeks that followed, and then, on June 25, Lee would seize the initiative by beginning his Seven Days' campaign.

Opposite, top: The 5th New Hampshire Infantry, along with details from the 64th New York and the Irish Brigade, reinforce the upper bridge across the Chickahominy River for General Edwin Sumner's troops to cross. The bridge was key to warding off Federal defeat on the first day of fighting at Seven Pines.

Above: Gibson's battery near Fair Oaks, Va. Although they were ready and very much needed at Fair Oaks, the swollen river kept them out of action.

Opposite, bottom: Union forces retreat from the Chickahominy on June 29th as stores and supplies burn in the background. The regiment in the foreground is the 16th New York, which lost 228 men in the Seven Days' Battles. The high casualty rate was due in part to their straw hats, which made them conspicuous targets.

Right: Lieutenant George A. Custer of the Fifth U.S. Cavalry wades across the Chickahominy. Drawing by Alfred Waud.

Top left: A Massachusetts Battery under Fitz-John Porter prepares to fire on Rebels across the Chickahominy. On June 26 Lee attacked Porter's corps, which was separated from the rest of McClellan's army by the swollen river. The Seven Days' Battles had begun the day before.

Top center: Union batteries fire at Confederate troops near Gaines's Mills on June 27. Lee had counted on Jackson's troops as part of the initial assault on the 26th, but Jackson, exhausted from the Valley Campaign, arrived late. As a result, Porter's troops repulsed the Rebels on the first day. Several Confederate attacks on the 27th failed as well, but the Rebels

finally broke through Union lines. Meanwhile, to the South of Porter's position, clever maneuvers by the Rebels led McClellan to believe he was outnumbered. In reality, his force was more than twice as large as the Confederate force on the south side of the river.

Top right: The battle at Savage Station on June 29, which began as an attack on the retreating Union army.

Above: Gen. Philip Kearney's division at the battle of White Oak Swamp on June 30.

Right: Another view of the battle at White Oak Swamp.

These pine grow near my first battery. B. 6

Slocum's Artillery engaged with the enemy on the Charles City Road. (Sevin

(fighting) The 16th U.S. Reg't as support.

Top: Union artillery face the Confederates on the Charles City Cross Roads on June 30. An engraving of a similar picture appeared in the August 9 issue of *Harper's Weekly*.

Opposite: The Battle of Malvern Hill on July 1, the last day of the Seven Days' Campaign. The battle ended after repeated Rebel attacks were cut down by Union artillery. In the previous seven days, nearly 20,000 Confederates and some 11,000 Union troops had been killed or wounded.

Above, left: Union gunboats on the James River shell Confederates during the Battle of Malvern Hill. After the battle, General Kearny reportedly wanted to push on to Richmond. Upon hearing of McClellan's orders to retreat, he responded that "such an order can only be prompted by cowardice or treason."

Above, right: Union and Confederate artillery clash at White Oak Swamp. Although Lee did not win a decisive victory during the Seven Days' Campaign, the key objective had been met: the enemy was demoralized and in retreat.

CONFRONTING SLAVERY

Above: A Southern slave auction. When the war began, roughly 4 million Americans lived in slavery.

Opposite: Five generations of slaves on a plantation in Beaufort, South Carolina. In 1861 only a minority of Northerners advocated abolition. By 1862, however, a growing number of Unionists were recognizing the importance of slavery to the Confederate war effort: with blacks working the fields and mines, whites were free to fight. Thus Northerners increasingly began advocating the destruction of slavery for military as well as moral reasons.

Right: Horace Greeley, founder and editor of *The New York Tribune*. On August 22 Greeley published an open letter asserting that abolition should be a chief aim of the war. Lincoln replied that he wished "all men everywhere could be free," but that his primary duty was still the salvation of the Union. "If I could save the Union without freeing any slave I would do it," he wrote. "If I could save it by freeing all the slaves I would do it; and if I could save it by freeing some and leaving others alone, I would also do that." Although few Americans knew it, Lincoln had already drafted a proclamation, which, in essence, reflected the last of the three strategies mentioned in the letter.

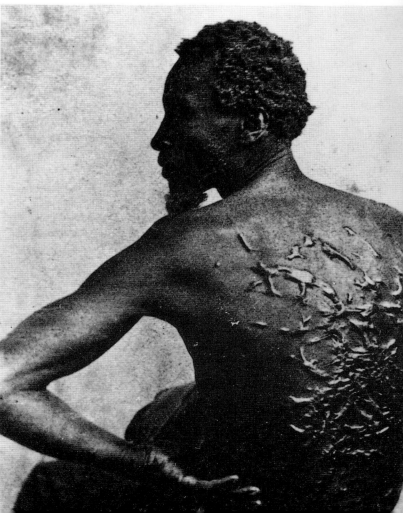

Opposite, top: A Union relief agency distributes clothing to displaced slaves in New Bern, North Carolina, after the seizure of the town. Lincoln initiated the destruction of slavery when, on August 6, 1861, he authorized the seizure of slaves as part of the war effort.

Opposite, bottom left: Assistant engineers of the Army of the Potomac. ''I came to fight for the restoration of the Union . . . not to free the niggers,'' wrote one Union soldier in 1861. But Northern soldiers, like the North as a whole, gradually began to favor abolition, particularly after blacks showed their courage on the battlefield.

Opposite, right: A slave, scarred from repeated whippings. Pictures like this refuted the Southern argument that slaves were better off than white factory workers in the North.

Above: Union soldiers outside the office of a Virginia slave dealer.

Right: Members of the 7th New York Militia early in the war.

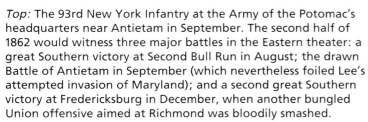

Top: The 93rd New York Infantry at the Army of the Potomac's headquarters near Antietam in September. The second half of 1862 would witness three major battles in the Eastern theater: a great Southern victory at Second Bull Run in August; the drawn Battle of Antietam in September (which nevertheless foiled Lee's attempted invasion of Maryland); and a second great Southern victory at Fredericksburg in December, when another bungled Union offensive aimed at Richmond was bloodily smashed.

Above, right: The Brooklyn 14th Regiment clashes with Confederate cavalrymen at Antietam. When the battle was over, nearly 5000 soldiers were dead and more than 18,000 were injured – several thousand fatally. Although the battle was a virtual draw, the Union had performed well enough to at least give the appearance of victory. Five days after the battle, Lincoln announced the Emancipation Proclamation.

Above, left: Union artillery under General Burnside in the Battle of Fredericksburg.

Opposite: Confederate casualties in the Battle of Fredericksburg. The pickets were killed when they came upon Union soldiers building a bridge across the Rappahannock River. The sketch is by artist-correspondent A.R. Waud.

Above: Union infantrymen march into battle at Fredericksburg which ended in brutal defeat for the North.

Left: An Arthur Lumley sketch of Union General Alfred Pleasonton leading his men through Warrington, Va., during the three-month interlude of desultory campaigning that separated the battles of Antietam and Fredericksburg.

Above, right: A drawing by A.R. Waud shows the railroad bridge at Fredericksburg.

Opposite, left: A Brady portrait of General McClellan and his wife. McClellan's failure to press his advantage at Antietam led to his replacement by Ambrose Burnside.

Opposite, right: Union soldiers push through the cornfield at Antietam.

Below: Confederate troops build makeshift fortifications at Manassas before the Second Battle of Bull Run. In August, General John Pope, head of the newly created Army of Virginia, began advancing toward Manassas, the objective again being the conquest of Richmond. Initially, the Confederates were outnumbered 3 to 1, but midway through the first full day of fighting General James Longstreet arrived with 30,000 reinforcements. Unaware of Longstreet's arrival, Pope pressed on the following day. The Confederates pushed the Federals back more than a mile before nightfall, and on September 1 Pope ordered a retreat to Washington.

Opposite: General Sigel's Corps at the Second Battle of Bull Run. The Union suffered 16,000 casualties during the battle, including the deaths of Generals J.J. Stevens and Philip Kearney.

Right: General Joseph Hooker, who replaced Burnside after the disaster at Fredericksburg.

Opposite, top: The Battle of Antietam. Some 45,000 Confederate and 75,000 Union troops took part in the fighting, which was concentrated in three distinct areas: the cornfield, a sunken wagon road later called "Bloody Lane," and a stone bridge.

Above: Union troops cross the bridge at Antietam Creek, now called Burnside Bridge. McClellan had ordered Burnside to cross the creek so that he might divert some of Lee's forces. For three hours 500 Rebel sharpshooters stopped Burnside's 13,000 men cold. In the early afternoon regiments from Pennsylvania and New York finally took the bridge, but the Rebels prevented Burnside from continuing his advance.

Right: Confederates cross the Potomac, midway between Harper's Ferry and Washington, before the Battle of Antietam.

Opposite, bottom: Second Battle of Bull Run. After the battle, the two sides agreed to a temporary truce for the purposes of collecting the wounded and burying the dead. One Union soldier later recalled how he and five other soldiers lay in a tent naked, each having had at least one leg amputated. "Our condition was horrible in the extreme . . . Our bodies became afflicted with loathsome sores, and – horror indescribable! – maggots found lodging in wounds and sores, and we were helpless. . . ."

Left: Residents of Sharpsburg, Maryland, evacuate the town. Hoping to win support in Maryland, Lee had ordered his troops to respect citizen's rights. When the Confederates occupied the town of Frederick on September 7 he made sure no food or supplies were taken without payment or any citizens mistreated. He even banned enthusiastic expressions of Southern pride, reprimanding one soldier who had ridden through the streets chanting Davis's name. Nevertheless, few Maryland men joined the Confederate cause.

Opposite, bottom: The bridge at Antietam Creek.

Below: The ''Irish Brigade,'' made up of men from Massachusetts and New York, drive Confederates from the cornfield near Sharpsburg. The Battle of Antietam opened in the cornfield and surged back and forth across it through the morning hours. Later, according to witnesses, corpses lay in great rows between the stalks, while the stalks themselves looked as if they had been ''struck by a storm of bloody hail.''

Opposite, top: Some of the wounded receive attention after the Battle of Antietam. Longstreet later wrote that it was ''heart-rending to see how Lee's army had been slashed by the day's fighting.''

Opposite, bottom: Confederates burn Samuel Mumma's property during the Battle of Antietam. Rebels feared the Yankees might take cover inside the thick-walled house.

Right: An Alfred Waud sketch made at Antietam shows Rebel troops in the West Woods repelling an attack by Sumner's corps on the Confederate left flank.

Below: Corpses lie in ''Bloody Lane'' after the Battle of Antietam. Total American casualties at Antietam exceeded all those suffered in the War of 1812, the Mexican War and the Spanish-American war.

Opposite, left: Lincoln meets with McClellan in the general's tent after the Battle of Antietam. McClellan believed he had fought ''a masterpiece,'' but few observers agreed with him.

Opposite, right: Signal Station on Elk Mountain, Maryland, overlooking the battlefield at Antietam.

Right: Soldiers of the Army of the Potomac salute McClellan after his dismissal in November. Despite his flaws as a battlefield commander, many soldiers loved him. Popular with Northern Democrats because of his conservative stance regarding slavery, he would challenge Lincoln for the Presidency.

Below: A wagon train crosses the pontoon bridge on the Rappahannock River, below Fredericksburg.

Previous pages: The Battle of Fredericksburg.

Opposite, top: Confederate troops pose for a Northern photographer on a bridge in Fredericksburg.

Left: Confederate fortifications on Marye's Heights behind Fredericksburg.

Above: Union engineers under General Burnside build a pontoon bridge across the Rappahannock before the Battle of Fredericksburg.

Right: Confederate corpses lie at the foot of Marye's Heights. During the Battle of Fredericksburg, Union soldiers charged this wall seven times without success. Five months later, during the Chancellorsville campaign, Federals under John Sedgwick finally managed to storm over the wall. This photograph was taken not long after their successful charge.

128

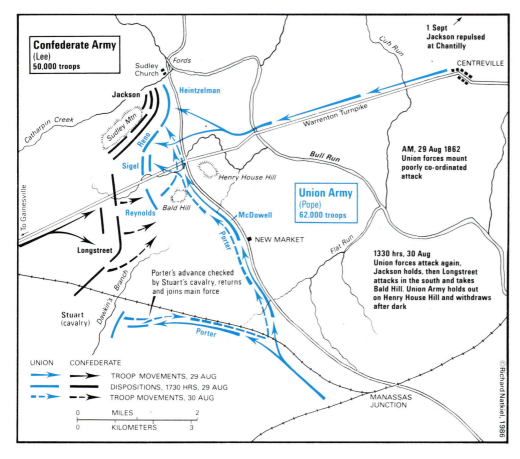

Above: Map of Second Bull Run.

Below, left: Map of Antietam.

Right: Amputees and other wounded soldiers at Marye's Heights.

Below, center: Confederate caisson wagons and horses lie in a ditch on

Marye's Heights after being destroyed by siege guns of a Massachusetts battery.

Opposite, bottom right: A sketch by Arthur Lumley of Union soldiers sacking Fredericksburg during the battle. *The New York Illustrated News*, refused to print it because of its unfavorable depiction of Yankees.

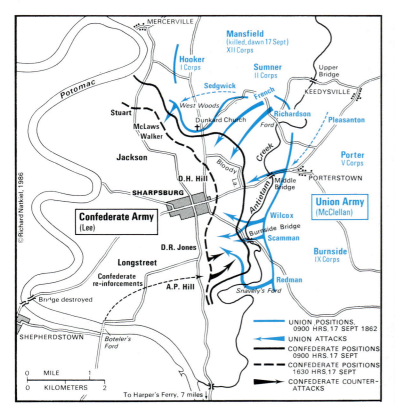

"– that we here highly resolve that these dead shall not have died in vain –"

Abraham Lincoln, November 1863

Heavy rains during the early months of 1863 severely limited the mobility of both armies. Grant, in particular, was hampered by the soggy ground west of the Mississippi near Vicksburg. Week after week, throughout the winter, he tried unsuccessfuly to move his army east of the river so he could launch an assault against the strategically vital city without having to face its powerful batteries head-on.

Grant's stalled operation became yet another reason for Northern discouragement as men who had visited his camp returned with news of the army's difficulties. In April, Grant proposed another plan: while Union gunboats and supplies floated downriver, past the Vicksburg batteries, the infantry would march along the west shore and rendezvous with the vessels below the city. The plan was extremely daring, but it worked.

Over the next few weeks Grant's army fought and won four battles east of Vicksburg. By mid-May the Federals were heading west again, and on May 17 Grant ordered an assault on Vicksburg itself. The situation of the Rebel forces defending the city was now exceedingly grim, but they would not yield, and in the end Grant was forced to settle in for a siege.

While Grant's army was on the march south of Vicksburg in early May, a major battle was taking place near Chancellorsville, Virginia. The battle ended in stunning defeat for the Union, but the Confederates also suffered serious losses in the course of the fighting. Among the 13,000 Rebel casualties was the South's second-best general, Stonewall Jackson.

The loss of Jackson notwithstanding, the victory at Chancellorsville gave Lee and his army new momentum. Brimming with confidence, the Army of Northern Virginia launched its second invasion of the North, and by late June, Rebel and Union troops were converging on the little town of Gettysburg, Pennsylvania. Here, during the first three days of July, they would fight the bloodiest and most famous battle of the war.

The Union victory at Gettysburg, the simultaneous surrender of Vicksburg, and a failing economy all but crippled the South. In the North, meanwhile, the Union victories carried enormous political consequences. Throughout the first half of 1863 Northern democrats had been using news of Federal military failures to fuel the fires of anti-war sentiment. The mid-year victories changed all that. The Republicans, it appeared, had not led the North into a quagmire after all.

Yet the victories did not completely unify the North. Ten days after the Battle of Gettysburg anti-draft riots erupted in New York City. The rioters, primarily members of the Irish

Previous pages: Beleagured Union troops try to hold off advancing Rebels who have outflanked them at Chancellorsville.

Left: A Union battery careers to the front during a skirmish in Virginia in September 1863.

Opposite top left: Union troops watch their batteries shell distant Rebel rifle pits near the Rappahannock in June 1863.

Opposite top right: An Irish newspaper offers frontline news reports from Vicksburg.

Opposite: A scene of the mist-shrouded 1863 Battle of Lookout Mountain, fought near Chattanooga.

working class, felt they had little to gain from a Union victory: they had, after all, reaped few benefits from the Northern industrial economy, and they felt they would face even greater difficulties if hordes of ex-slaves entered the competition for jobs. For three days a mob of 50,000 stormed through the streets of New York, burning buildings and attacking blacks. Ultimately, militia and troops returning from Gettysburg were called in to subdue the rioters.

The New York riot, and similar disturbances in other Northern cities, foreshadowed problems that would plague America in the late nineteenth and twentieth centuries. In the near-term, however, these problems were overshadowed by the unceasing brutality of the war. For the remainder of 1863 the Union armies would continue to take advantage of the Confederacy's weakened condition, but the Union's progress would be made at great cost, and Northerners could not help wondering whether such sacrifices would ultimately be justified.

IMPORTANT FROM AMERICA!!
Awful Slaughter at Vicksburg,
And Elsewhere,
The Bloody Conflict between the North & South
CONTINUED!

We regret to say that this unnatural war seems still to rush upon the unhappy Yanky with fearful impetuosity, so as to stun the entire population and saturate the States of America with blood, by sacrificing the lives of hundreds of thousands of honest men, at the whim or caprice of a few noxious individuals. Federal accounts state that the siege still continues, —and, that the incredible number of 3,600 bombs were thrown into the city of Vicksburg in an hour! The streets are ploughed up with shot and shell, and that the inhabitants dwell in caves which they have excavated in the sides of the Bluff!

In the force under Banks and Sheridan there was a battalion of Negroes, who are said to have fought well. They suffered terribly, for out of a regiment of 900, 600 were killed or wounded in an hour!

The Prize Court at Key West has laid down the law of confiscation so as to insure the condemnation of every British Ship a Federal vessel may seize,—'Any vessel bound to Nassau, with the intention of sailing from thence to a blockaded port, is liable to condemnation." As the prize court constitutes itself sole judge of the intention, and as Matamoros has been, de facto blockaded, all British vessels bound for that port will, of course, be at once condemned. The Key west correspondent of the New-York Herald has good reason to say that "nowhere else is prize law rigidly enforced, vessels being condemned at the rate of two each week."

Although 49,688 emigrants had arrived in New York from Ireland since the first of January, 1863, and though the negroes are said to be the "best hope of restoring the Union," the enrollment is being enforced.

Queenstown, Saturday,—The following is the latest "correspondence" from Vicksburg. One regiment only, if it tried from Vicksburg, commanded by Colonel William M. Stone, by almost superhuman efforts, and after immense loss, planted its colours on the rebel rampart. There is remained all day long, the self and barely demanding aid, until at nightfall, after having been exposed all day to a destructive fire, the lieutenant-colonel and 15 men only remained and they were taken in great triumph to Vicksburg. Every man who entered the fort in the morning was killed or wounded except Colonel Stone were borne to the rear whilst on the blockers, loudly calling for reinforcements. It was a stupid blunder, or worse, to turn the works at all, it needs not a military eye to discover that it is impossible to lead men over an almost undefended twenty feet high, with ditches three foot to twelve feet deep. It was doubtless, necessary that the experiment should be tried. It lost power a costly one. Twenty-three hundred killed and wounded is a fearful loss.

The northerns are evidently constructing a new line of works between the outer line opposed to us and the city. While the charge was being made on the 22nd some of our sharp-shooters, posted in the trees overlooking the fortifications, could plainly see commatando and white men digging for dear life.

OUR LOSSES

I regret to learn that Colonel Abbott, of the 36th Iowa, was killed on the 22nd instant. He was a brave officer, and his loss is seriously regretted. In the battle of Champion's Hill, on the 16th, instant, the tenth Iowa lost, killed, wounded, and missing, one hundred and sixty-two men. Among the killed were three commissioned officers and 7 wounded. In the recent charges on the fortifications the twenty-second Iowa, lost two hundred and fifty men; General Benton's Brigade, three hundred and sixty-eight; General Carr's division, five hundred; General Blair's division, five hundred and fifty; General Steele's division, heavily, estimated at hundred; General Osterhaus' division two hundred, estimated; and General Smith's three hundred and fifty, estimated. This is rather under than over the estimate.

GENERAL BANKS.

To-day there has been vigorous cannonading at intervals from batteries on the right and left of the railroad. A misdirected shot fell in our own ranks killing three soldiers of the thirty-second Ohio, not seriously wounding as many more.

Over one hundred women and children have been killed by our bombardment.

New-York, June 14—General Banks floatishly reports that the conduct of the Negro troops has been most praiseworthy, and there is no longer any doubt

that the Government will find in the Negroes effective supporters.

General Banks' loss from the 28rd to the 30th ult., was 1,800 men, including many of his oldest officers.

General Sherman has died of his wounds.

General Neal Dow is also dangerously wounded.

ANOTHER BATTLE.

Three brigades of Federal Cavalry, and 3,000 infantry crossed the Rappahannock on Tuesday at Beverley Ford, and had a severe engagement with General Stuart's cavalry, lasting all day, when the Confederates received heavy infantry reinforcements, and the Federals recrossed the river bringing away their dead and wounded. Sharp firing was kept up from the confederate rifle pits during the evening, and 40 of the Federals were killed or wounded. A portion of Federal land and naval forces at Yorktown, made an incursion into King William County, Virginia, via the Mattapony River. On the 4th inst. a Foundry at Ayleton, with all its machinery, several mi'ls, and large quantities of grain, were destroyed, and many horses, mules, and cattle were captured. The expedition returned to Yorktown the following day.

The agricultural resources of the Yazoo country are described as being most abundant.

John F. Nugent and Co., Steam-Machine Printers, 35, New-Row West, Dublin. N.B.—No connection with any other person of the name.

STONE'S RIVER AND VICKSBURG

Below: Grant's headquarters on the Mississippi River, about 10 miles north of Vicksburg. Here, in January 1863, Grant began preparing his army of 50,000 for a campaign against Vicksburg.

Above, right: A Union vessel begins a dredging operation at the head of the Vicksburg Canal. Grant had hoped to bypass the batteries on the Mississippi at Vicksburg by creating an alternate water route. In the end, all attempts to dredge the canal or dig a new one failed.

Above left: Southern refugees near Vicksburg. When the Union Army began shelling the city women and children fled to the outskirts of town. Many took cover in caves.

Left: Ulysses S. Grant. As the winter of 1862-3 dragged on Grant continued efforts to bypass the Vicksburg batteries in spite of heavy rains which flooded the swamps north and west of the city. ''Troops could scarcely find dry ground on which to pitch their tents,'' he recalled, adding that his men were struck by malaria, measles and smallpox. By early spring some Northerners had lost faith in him and were calling for his removal. But Lincoln forgave Grant for these temporary setbacks. Although the two had yet to meet, the President saw in his general the character traits that would ultimately lead to success: iron will, great courage, an ability to stay calm under pressure and a willingness to take risks.

Left: William Tecumseh Sherman. In December, under orders from Grant, Sherman led an expedition from Memphis down the Mississippi toward Vicksburg. On the 29th Sherman's four divisions charged Chickasaw bluffs, where 14,000 Rebel troops were entrenched. Although the Federals outnumbered the Rebels two-to-one, the Confederate's position on high ground gave them the advantage.

Below: The business district of Vicksburg, Mississippi.

Opposite, top and bottom: The Battle of Stone's River. On October 30, 1862, Union General William S. Rosecrans took command of the Army of the Cumberland. His immediate objective was to push the Rebels out of central Tennessee. Two months later, on New Year's Eve day, Rosecrans's troops clashed with Confederates under Braxton Bragg near Stone's River on the outskirts of Murfreesboro. The Confederates had opened the battle and had quickly gained the upper hand. But Rosecrans was unshaken, even after a cannonball howled past his head and decapitated his chief of staff, who was riding next to him, and with the help of Philip Sheridan, among others, Rosecrans managed to hold the Union position. The Rebels attacked again on January 2, but without success. The following night they retreated. Each side had lost nearly a third of its men, and casualties in Sheridan's division approached 40 percent.

Above: Shops in Vicksburg. As the Union encircled Vicksburg it cut off supply lines to the town and the army. ''The enemy was limited in supplies of food, men, and munitions of war,'' Grant recalled later. ''These could not last.''

Opposite: Union artillery fire on Vicksburg.

Above, right: Rear Admiral David Dixon Porter who, working with Grant and Sherman, played a key role in the Vicksburg campaign. He ran a fleet of transports down the Mississippi past Vicksburg's guns on April 16, and two week's later Grant's army crossed the river.

Right: A Confederate woman prays inside the cave that has become her temporary home outside of Vicksburg. ''In the midst of all this carnage and commotion,'' wrote a Vicksburg woman in her diary, ''birds are singing . . . flowers are in perfection . . . and the garden [is] bright and gay . . . all save the spirit of man seems divine.''

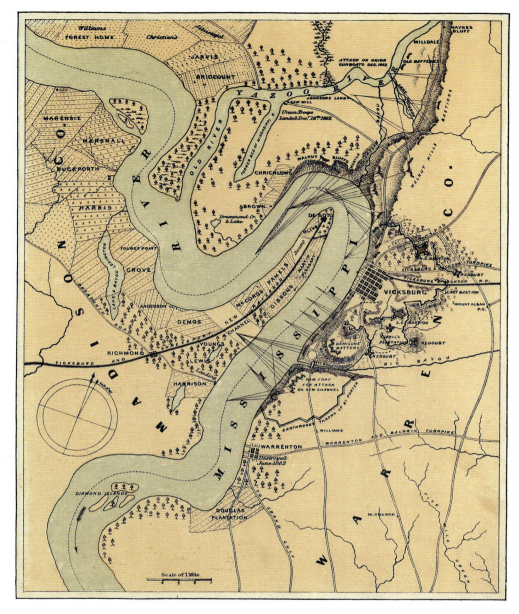

Left: This Army topographical map shows Vicksburg and its surrounding area and emphasizes the siting of the Rebel batteries.

Below: After taking Jackson, Mississippi, Grant wheeled west toward Vicksburg. Confederate General John Pemberton tried to stop him at Champion's Hill (shown here), but Grant's momentum was now irresistible.

Opposite, top: The Siege of Vicksburg.

Opposite, bottom: Grant's field headquarters near Vicksburg.

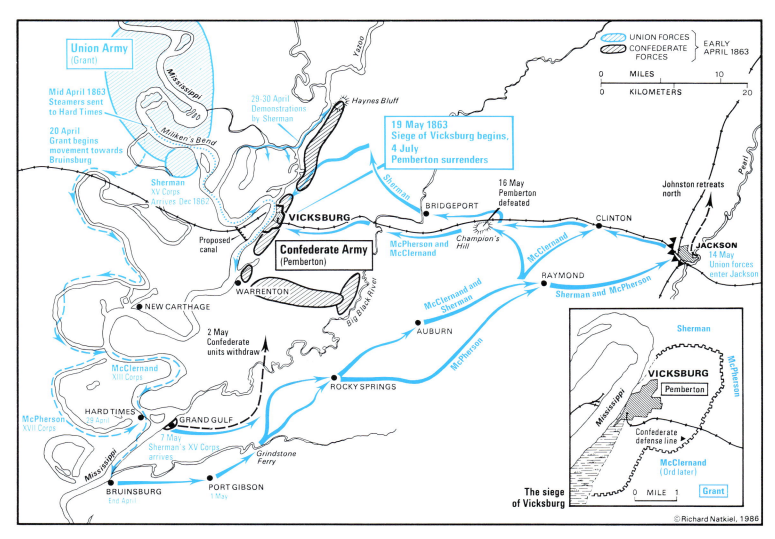

Union Army (Grant)

Mid April 1863 Steamers sent to Hard Times

20 April Grant begins movement towards Bruinsburg

Sherman XV Corps Arrives Dec 1862

29-30 April Demonstrations by Sherman

Haynes Bluff

Yazoo

UNION FORCES
CONFEDERATE FORCES

EARLY APRIL 1863

MILES 0 10
KILOMETERS 0 20

19 May 1863 Siege of Vicksburg begins, 4 July Pemberton surrenders

Sherman

BRIDGEPORT

16 May Pemberton defeated

Johnston retreats north

Pearl

CLINTON

VICKSBURG

Proposed canal

Miliken's Bend

Mississippi

Confederate Army (Pemberton)

McPherson and McClernand

Champion's Hill

McClernand

JACKSON

14 May Union forces enter Jackson

WARRENTON

Big Black River

McClernand and Sherman

RAYMOND

Sherman and McPherson

NEW CARTHAGE

2 May Confederate units withdraw

AUBURN

McPherson

McClernand XIII Corps

ROCKY SPRINGS

HARD TIMES 29 April

GRAND GULF

McPherson XVII Corps

7 May Sherman's XV Corps arrives

Grindstone Ferry

Mississippi

BRUINSBURG End April

PORT GIBSON 1 May

Sherman

VICKSBURG

Pemberton

McPherson

Mississippi

Confederate defense line

McClernand (Ord later)

Grant

0 MILE 1

The siege of Vicksburg

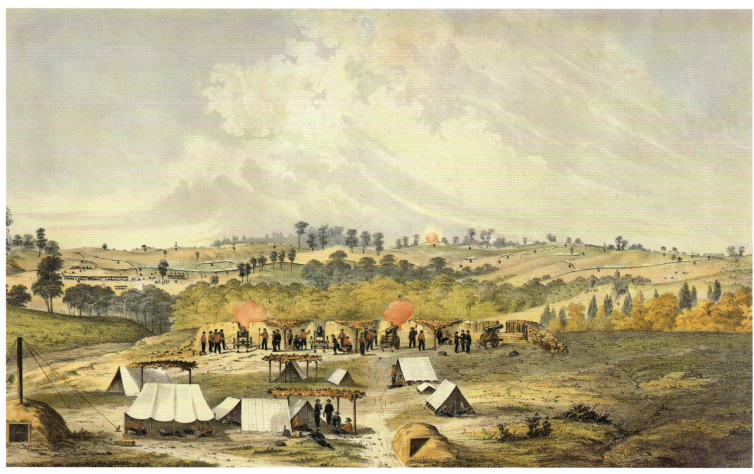

Right: Grant, at his field headquarters outside of Vicksburg on July 3, reads General Pemberton's message requesting terms of surrender.

Below, far right: Band of the 8th New York State Militia. Bands on both sides provided an important emotional outlet. The night before the Battle of Stone's River, Bragg's and Rosecrans's forces were treated to a battle of the bands. After trying to outdo each other with songs like "Dixie" and "Yankee Doodle," both sides began playing "Home Sweet Home." Soon, forgetting their differences for a few brief moments, the enemies began singing together.

Below: One of the "Louisiana Tigers," a brigade with a reputation for violence on and off the battlefield.

Below, center: Union troops prepare to march.

Overleaf: The Siege of Vicksburg.

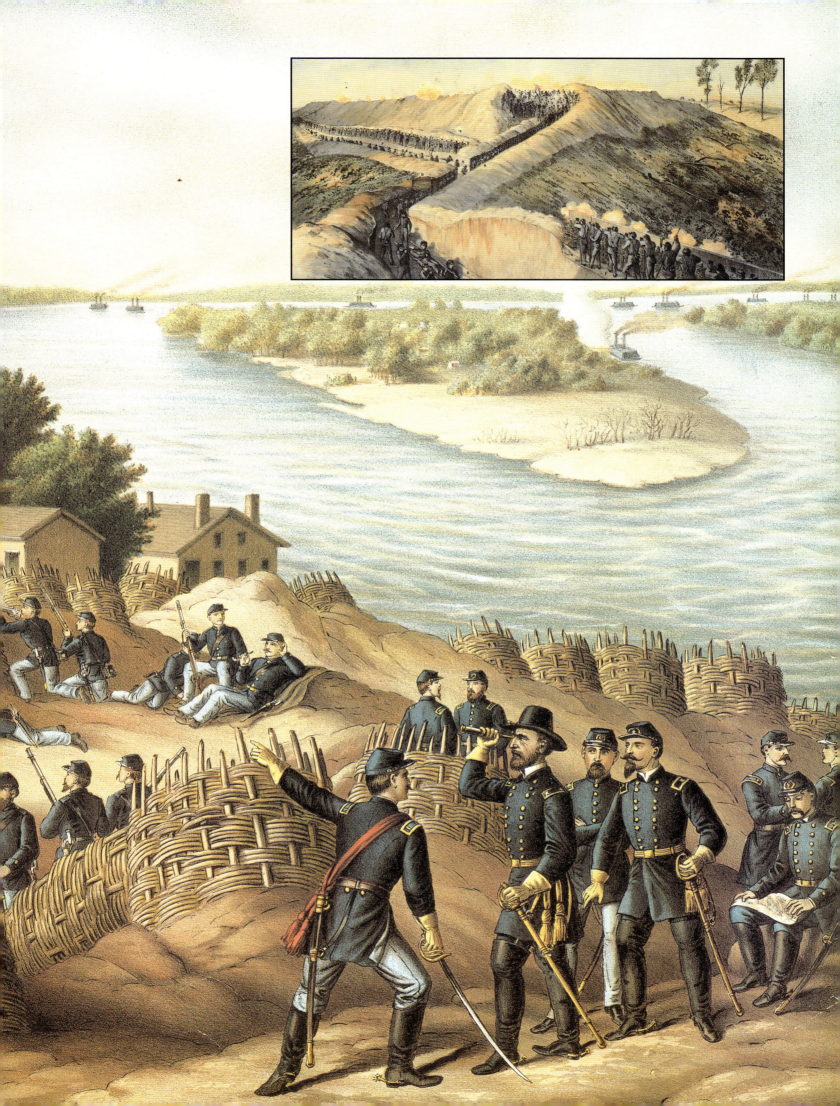

CHANCELLORSVILLE AND GETTYSBURG

Above and opposite: Union forces defend Cemetery Hill during the Battle of Gettysburg. In the spring of 1863, Lee proposed to follow up his stunning victory at Chancellorsville with another invasion of the North. Longstreet recommended instead an expedition to help Bragg push Rosecrans out of Tennessee, reasoning that such a move would force Grant to abandon his siege of Vicksburg. Unfortunately for the South, Lee's thinking prevailed. He argued that Grant must soon abandon his hopeless siege anyway, while an invasion of the North would provide new food supplies for the starving Rebels, would reduce the threat to Richmond by moving the war away from the Confederate capital and, finally, would strengthen the resolve of anti-war Northerners and might even induce England and France to recognize the Confederacy. So, on June 3, having received approval for his plan, Lee reorganized his army into three corps under Longstreet, A.P. Hill and Richard S. Ewell, and a short time later the invasion was begun. It would take Lee to Gettysburg and catastrophe.

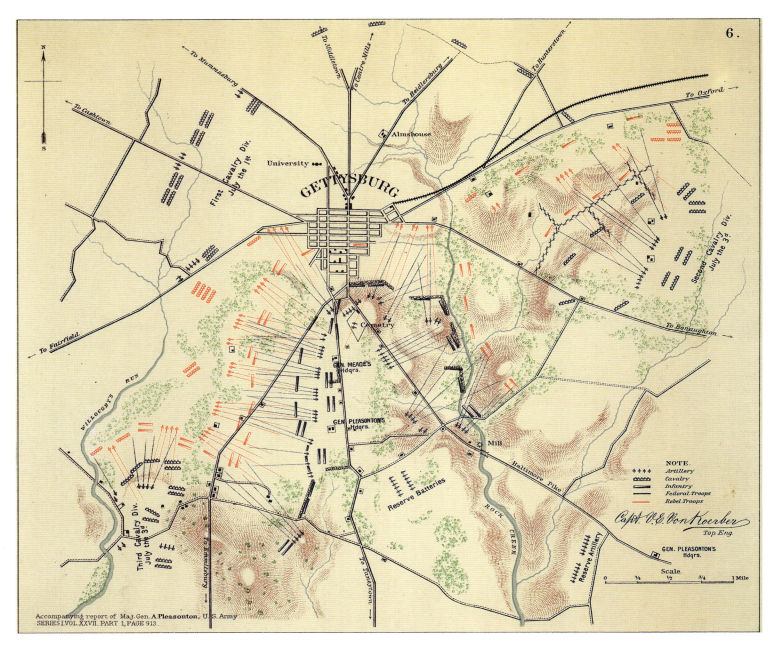

6.

To Mummasburg · To Middletown · To Centre Mills · To Heidlersburg · To Hunterstown · To Oxford

To Cashtown

Almshouse

University

GETTYSBURG

First Cavalry Div. July the 1st

Second Cavalry Div. July the 3d.

To Fairfield

Cemetry

To Bonaughton

GEN. MEADE'S Hddqrs.

WILLOUGHBY'S RUN

GEN PLEASONTON'S Hddqrs.

Mill

Baltimore Pike

Reserve Batteries

ROCK CREEK

NOTE.
++++ Artillery
Cavalry
Infantry
Federal Troops
Rebel Troops

Capt. O.E.Von Koerber
Top. Eng.

Third Cavalry Div. July the 3d.

Reserve Artillery

GEN. PLEASONTON'S Hddqrs.

Scale.
0   ¼   ½   ¾   1 Mile

Accompanying report of Maj. Gen. A. Pleasonton, U.S. Army
SERIES I. VOL. XXVII. PART 1, PAGE 913.

The Death of Reynolds Gettysburg

Opposite, top: A map of Gettysburg, showing the locations of artillery, infantry and cavalry on both sides during the three-day battle.

Opposite, bottom left: Union General John F. Reynolds falls from his horse after being hit by a Confederate's bullet at Gettysburg.

Opposite, bottom right: Stonewall Jackson at Chancellorsville. Although the Rebels won the battle, it may have cost them the war: not only was the irreplaceable Jackson accidentally shot by a Confederate soldier, the magnitude of the Southern victory at Chancellorsville persuaded Lee that his army was now strong enough to invade the North, a fatal error.

Right: Lee and Jackson meet for the last time at Chancellorsville.

Below: "Pickett's Charge" at Gettysburg. On the third day of the battle, over Longstreet's objections, Lee ordered three divisions, one under Major General George Pickett, to prepare to charge the center of the Union line. On Longstreet's reluctant orders 15,000 men emerged from the woods and began marching toward the Union army. Met by withering Union fire, whole groups of them were blown apart by single shells, while the Federals shouted "Fredericksburg!"

Opposite, top: The Battle of Chancellorsville. On May 2 Lee ordered Jackson to attack the Union's right flank, which was spread out east of Chancellorsville. Jackson's men surprised the Union soldiers as they were having dinner, and easily overtook them. When Union reinforcements finally halted this assault, Jackson decided to return briefly to his lines and prepare for another attack. As he rode into Confederate territory, nervous Rebel soldiers shot him, having mistaken him for the enemy.

Opposite, bottom: Men of the 14th New York set up camp between breastworks on the night of May 6 after their defeat at the Battle of Chancellorsville.

Above: The 2nd and 3rd Corps repel Jackson's assault in the top half of this drawing by A.R. Waud; the bottom half shows General Joseph Hooker's field headquarters near Chancellorsville.

Right: Major General George Meade replaced Hooker, who had been under a cloud since his defeat at Chancellorsville, as commander of the Army of the Potomac only days before the Battle of Gettysburg. Meade fought the battle admirably, but Lincoln was less pleased when Meade failed to pursue the Rebels as they retreated. Had he done so, he might have delivered a fatal blow to the Confederacy.

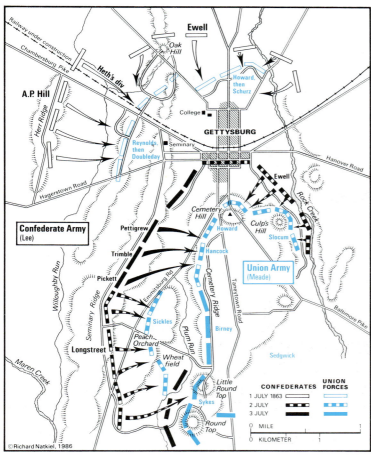

Opposite, top: An artist's version of Jackson being wounded at Chancellorsville. In fact, Jackson was wounded behind his own lines.

Opposite, bottom left: Union and Confederate positions at the Battle of Gettysburg.

Opposite, bottom right: Robert E. Lee.

Above: Lee's army crosses the Potomac on June 11.

Below: Invasion of Pennsylvania. The Columbia Railroad Bridge burns in the background.

Opposite: Union lines at Gettysburg under attack by General Edward Johnson's division on July 2. Wolf and Culp's Hills are on the right, Cemetery Hill in the center and Powers Hill, headquarters of General Slocum, on the left.

Below: A Union encampment at Culpeper, Virginia, in 1863.

Right: A Union doctor prepares to amputate the leg of a wounded soldier at Gettysburg. The battle was by far the bloodiest of the war, resulting in 51,000 casualties – 28,000 for the Confederates and 23,000 for the Union.

Above, below and opposite bottom: Scenes from the long, drawn-out, and bloody Battle of Gettysburg.

Opposite, top: Battery B., 2nd US Artillery at Gettysburg.

Above: Confederate soldiers stand defiant after being captured at Gettysburg.

Left: General George Pickett. After the Union turned back Pickett's charge Lee ordered him to rally his division for a renewed assault. ''I have no division now,'' the 38-year-old general responded. After the war Pickett recalled bitterly how Lee had his division ''slaughtered at Gettysburg.''

Opposite, top: The Battle of Gettysburg.

Opposite, bottom: Union dead at Gettysburg. The shoes of the dead soldiers were taken by Rebels.

Opposite, top: The Battle of Gettysburg.

Opposite, bottom: Lincoln, seated to the immediate left of the man in the top hat, prepares to deliver the Gettysburg Address. After the ceremony, Lincoln told a friend his speech had been ''a flat failure.''

Above: This series of engravings appeared in the December 5 issue of *Frank Leslie's Illustrated Newspaper*, along with a report on the dedication ceremony. Like Lincoln himself, few papers at the time recognized the eloquence and timeless power of the speech. One paper reported simply that ''the President also spoke,'' emphasizing instead the two-hour speech by Edward Everett, former governor of Massachusetts and a nationally known orator.

Right: A fallen Rebel sharpshooter at Devil's Den, Gettysburg.

THE CHATTANOOGA CAMPAIGN

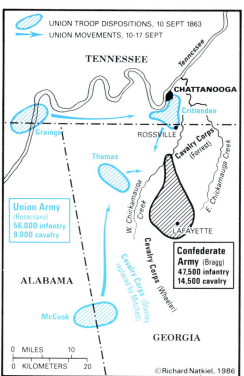

UNION TROOP DISPOSITIONS, 10 SEPT 1863
UNION MOVEMENTS, 10-17 SEPT

TENNESSEE

Tennessee

CHATTANOOGA

Crittenden

Grainge

ROSSVILLE

Cavalry Corps (Forrest)

Thomas

W. Chickamauga Creek

E. Chickamauga Creek

Union Army
(Rosecrans)
56,000 infantry
9,000 cavalry

LAFAYETTE

Cavalry Corps
(Stanley
replaced by Mitchell)

ALABAMA

Confederate
Army (Bragg)
47,500 infantry
14,500 cavalry

McCook

GEORGIA

0 MILES 10
0 KILOMETERS 20

© Richard Natkiel, 1986

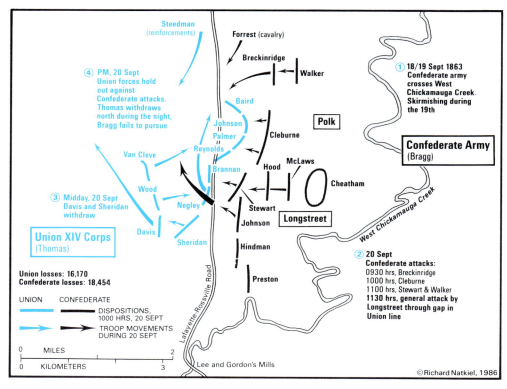

Steedman
(reinforcements)

Forrest (cavalry)

Breckinridge ← Walker

④ PM, 20 Sept
Union forces hold
out against
Confederate attacks.
Thomas withdraws
north during the night,
Bragg fails to pursue

Baird

Johnson
Palmer

Cleburne

Polk

Reynolds

Van Cleve

Brannan

Hood   McLaws

Cheatham

Wood

Negley

Stewart

Longstreet

③ Midday, 20 Sept
Davis and Sheridan
withdraw

Johnson

Davis

Sheridan

Hindman

Union XIV Corps
(Thomas)

Preston

Union losses: 16,170
Confederate losses: 18,454

① 18/19 Sept 1863
Confederate army
crosses West
Chickamauga Creek.
Skirmishing during
the 19th

Confederate Army
(Bragg)

West Chickamauga Creek

② 20 Sept
Confederate attacks:
0930 hrs, Breckinridge
1000 hrs, Cleburne
1100 hrs, Stewart & Walker
1130 hrs, general attack by
Longstreet through gap in
Union line

UNION	CONFEDERATE	
		DISPOSITIONS, 1000 HRS, 20 SEPT
		TROOP MOVEMENTS DURING 20 SEPT

0 MILES 2
0 KILOMETERS 3

Lafayette-Rossville Road

Lee and Gordon's Mills

© Richard Natkiel, 1986

Opposite: The Battle of Chickamauga. After the Battle of Stone's River, Bragg's and Rosecrans's armies had maintained static positions near each other in southern Tennessee. Finally, in June 1863, Rosecrans began his advance. By September 9 he had taken Chattagnooga. Ten days later the two armies faced off at Chickamauga Creek in northern Georgia.

Top: The armies clash at Chickamauga. The first day of fighting was fierce but indecisive.

Above: The positions of the two armies at Chickamauga.

CHICKAMAUGA.

Opposite, top: Union and Confederates advance toward each other at Chickamauga in this drawing by A.R. Waud.

Opposite, bottom: Part of the Confederate line in Chickamauga woods. Shortly before noon on the 20th the Rebels gained the upper hand when Longstreet, noticing a hole in the Union line, plowed through and scattered the Union's right flank. He then turned for a renewed attack on Thomas.

Right: General Thomas. With the help of reinforcements, he strengthened the Union line and held off several vicious Confederate assaults throughout the afternoon. His heroic performance earned him the nickname, "The Rock of Chickamauga."

Above: Major General George Thomas, left, and his men fend off the Rebels at Chickamauga. In spite of Thomas's resistance, the Union was forced to retreat; the Confederates had won the battle but had lost approximately 18,000 men in the process. "The dead were piled upon each other . . . like cord wood," one Rebel said later. Reeling from the heavy losses, Bragg failed to pursue Rosecrans, and the Union retained its position at Chattanooga.

Previous pages: The Battle of Missionary Ridge. After the Union retreat to Chattanooga, Bragg took up positions to the east, on Missionary Ridge and Lookout Mountain, and cut the enemy's supply line. Recognizing the Union army's precarious position, Lincoln ordered reinforcements for Rosecrans: 17,000 under Sherman and 20,000 under Hooker. Then, on October 17, he gave Grant overall command of these armies. Six days later Grant arrived in Chattanooga and quickly opened up a new supply line.

Opposite, top: The Battle of Missionary Ridge. On November 23 Thomas's army took a strategic position at Orchard's Knob in front of Missionary Ridge, and the following day Hooker seized Lookout Mountain. On November 25 Union soldiers began a charge up Missionary Ridge – without orders to do so. The charge seemed suicidal, but the Yankees were able to find cover in ravines along the side of the ridge and by late afternoon had driven the Rebels from their main position.

Opposite, bottom: Chattanooga, Tennessee, with Lookout Mountain in the distance.

Right: Union officers at the headquarters of General Hooker in Chattanooga.

Below: Missionary Ridge after the battle.

Left: Grant, lower left, and his staff on Lookout Mountain after winning the battle there. The success at Vicksburg convinced Lincoln that Grant was the general he had been searching for. The victory at Chattanooga reinforced Lincoln's faith, and the following March he made Grant commander of all Union armies.

Above: A view of Lookout Mountain from an encampment of the Army of the Cumberland outside Chattanooga.

Opposite, top: General Thomas's charge near Orchard Knob during the Battle of Chattanooga.

Opposite: The Battle of Lookout Mountain.

THE DRAFT

BATTLE OF
MILLIKEN'S BEND

Opposite: A mob attacks Union soldiers in St. Louis in 1861. From the start of the war the Union had to contend with civilian mobs as well as Confederate troops. When the North initiated a draft in 1863 a new wave of protests and violence erupted among poor Northerners, *below*, who felt they had little to gain from the war – especially since it had become a war for emancipation.

Above: Black Union troops clash with Rebels in the Battle of Milliken's Bend, just north of Vicksburg, in June 1863. "The bravery of the blacks in the battle . . . completely revolutionized the sentiment of the army with regard to the employment of negro troops," wrote a War Department official.

Right: A Northerner draws a number to determine whether he'll be drafted.

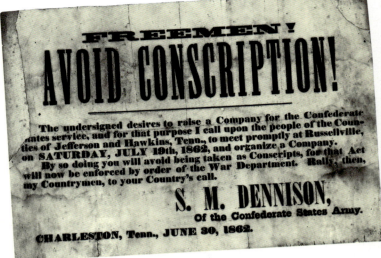

Left: A mob destroys a house in New York City during anti-draft rioting on July 13.

Above: A poster calling for the men of Jefferson and Hawkins counties in Tennessee to join the Confederate army and, *below,* a picture from a Northern recruiting poster.

Opposite, top: The Fort Pillow Massacre. On April 12, 1864, Confederates captured Fort Pillow, Tennessee, and then killed almost half the troops stationed there.

Opposite, bottom: The storming of Fort Wagner. On July 18, 1863, the all-black 54th Massachusetts led a brave, but fruitless charge against Fort Wagner in Charleston harbor.

Top: Militia fire on the anti-draft rioters in New York. On July 13, 1863, Irish mobs erupted in anger over the newly established draft. These laborers saw little reason to fight for the North, having gained little from the region's economic growth. Racial prejudice fueled their resentment, and blacks became a target of the mobs. Over the next few days, the mob – 50,000 strong – lynched more than a dozen blacks and burned a number of buildings, including the New York draft office, a black orphanage and the offices of the *New York Tribune.* The rioting did not end until police and Federal troops opened fire on the mob, killing at least 100 people. Countless people had been seriously injured during the four-day riot, the worst in the country's history.

Above: Black recruits march along Beekman Street in New York City.

Opposite, top: 1st U.S. Colored Infantry. Although the Navy had had some black sailors from the beginning, the war would be half over before blacks were accepted into the army. In July 1862 Congress passed a law authorizing the enrollment of blacks for any military service, but for the remainder of the year the army used blacks primarily as laborers. After the Emancipation Proclamation took effect in 1863 the War Department created a bureau specifically to recruit black troops. Racism remained widespread in the Union army throughout the war, but numerous letters from white troops reveal a drastic change in racial attitudes after 1863.

Opposite, bottom: The 26th U.S. Colored Volunteer Infantry on parade at Camp William Penn, Pennsylvania, in 1865. By the end of the war 166 black regiments had been organized.

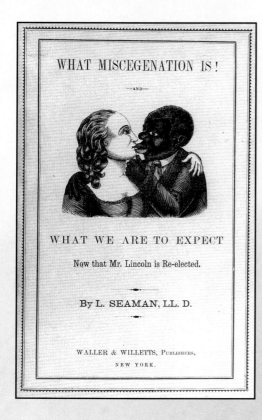

WHAT MISCEGENATION IS!

—AND—

WHAT WE ARE TO EXPECT

Now that Mr. Lincoln is Re-elected.

By L. SEAMAN, LL. D.

WALLER & WILLETTS, PUBLISHERS,
NEW YORK.

Opposite, left: The cover of a pamphlet written in 1863 and published the following year after Lincoln was re-elected. The word "miscegenation" was coined during the war by a journalist, David G. Croly. The prospect was viewed in the South as a profound threat to civilized society.

Opposite, right: Blacks build a stockade in Alexandria, Virginia.

Immediate right: Black Union soldier Charles Young.

Far right: John H. Lawson, a naval hero.

Below: Black troops at Yorktown, Virginia, in June 1862.

Opposite: A drawing mocking those who were opposing the war and seeking to avoid the draft: the original caption suggested that this was an appropriate costume for the "brave, stay-at-home 'light guard'."

Above, left: The Union defends herself against the Copperheads in a cartoon from 1863. Prior to the key Unions victories in 1863 Northern morale was low and anti-war sentiment flourished in some sections of the country. Groups began to meet in secret with the aim of finding ways to end the war. Eventually Clement L. Vallandigham, Ohio gubernatorial candidate and a Copperhead leader, was arrested and banished from the Union by Lincoln. The anti-war Democrats, often compared with poisonous copperhead snakes, embraced the name and began wearing lapel pins fashioned from copper pennies.

Above, right: A cartoon mocks those who would injure themselves to avoid the draft. A medical exemption was one of the few ways a Northerner could avoid the draft.

Below: A pair of illustrations, originally captioned "Sowing and Reaping," shows Southern women "hounding their men on to rebellion" (left) and rioting for bread (right). The war devastated the Southern economy and sparked uncontrollable inflation. By the end of 1863 Richmond merchants were charging upwards of $100 for a barrel of flour.

Above: A provost marshal (officer wearing sash) examines a soldier's furlough pass in Washington DC.

Below: Union soldiers search for arms in the home of a suspected Confederate sympathizer in Maryland.

Opposite, top: A Washington street scene focuses on men who failed to do their part in the war effort.

Opposite, bottom: Casualties from the Battle of Seven Pines gather in the streets of Richmond.

W. L. Sheppard

Opposite, top left: Southern children taunt a Northern sympathizer in this cartoon by Thomas Nast.

Opposite, top right: A Baltimore woman flaunts the insignia of the Confederacy in front of Union troops who are occupying the city.

Opposite, bottom: Southern women and slaves gather to receive their rations.

Above: The unsavory businessman in this picture was probably intended to represent those who engaged in trade with the enemy for no other reason than personal profit. Try as they might, neither side could stop such trade.

Above, right: Military fashion suggested during the Civil War.

Right: Confederate women make clothes for soldiers.

Opposite, top: A Southern clergyman donates church bells to the Confederate cause so they can be recast into cannon.

Opposite, bottom: Southern Unionists meet secretly to plot the overthrow of the Confederate government.

Below: A hospital volunteer writes a letter for an injured soldier in this drawing by Winslow Homer. The United States Sanitary Commission was the chief agency through which Northern women channeled volunteer efforts. A weak economy and a mentality that put the needs of states before those of the Confederacy hindered similar efforts in the South. The four Confederate states that did have formal relief agencies tended to help only their native sons.

Below, right: A want ad for a substitute. By hiring a substitute, wealthy men could avoid the draft. Among those who took advantage of this aspect of the draft law were Andrew Carnegie and J.P. Morgan. It was also possible to avoid an immediate draft, but not future drafts, by paying $3000.

Right: A cartoon from *Harper's Weekly.* The original caption read: "Richmond newsboy announcing the Rebel success!"

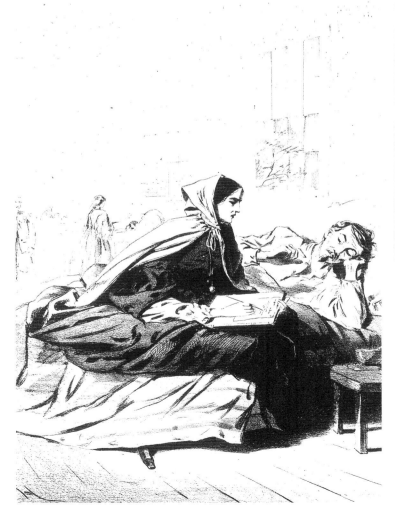

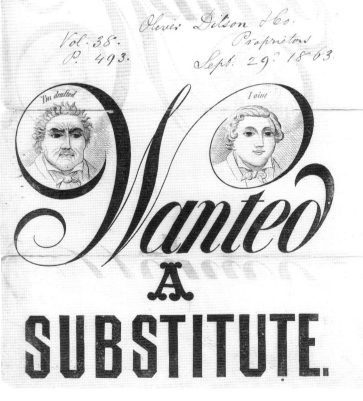

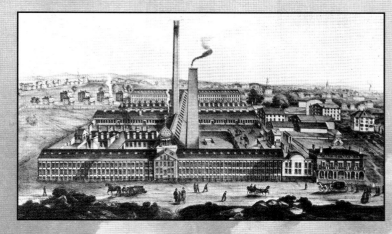

Below: A Southern cotton plantation. Lack of a diversified economy was a fatal weakness of the Confederacy.

Opposite: An iron company in Trenton, New Jersey. The iron industry in the North suffered slightly in the early years of the war, but by 1863 it was booming.

Above: The Colt gun factory in Hartford, Connecticut. The firearms industry was another beneficiary of wartime.

Right: The South Street Seaport in New York City was a bustling port during the war.

Left: The world's first oil well, drilled in Pennsylvania in 1859. Three years later, *The Scientific American* noted that the use of oil "for artificial illumination has spread over all parts of the civilized world. . . . The obtaining of it from the oil wells, the refining of it, the carrying of it to market and the export of it abroad, combine to form a new manufacturing and commercial business for America . . . which is the source of no small amount of wealth."

Bottom: A Southern railroad depot. At the outset of the war, the North had some 20,000 miles of railroad; the South only 9000.

Below: Soldiers guard a railroad bridge at Bull Run. As railroads became increasingly important to the war effort, they became prime military targets.

Right: The engine "Firefly" on a trestle of the Orange and Alexandria Railroad.

Left: A U.S. Military Railroads depot in City Point, Va. In 1864 the Union created The United States Military Railroads. In addition to maintaining captured railroads, the agency built new ones. By the end of the war it employed 25,000 men and was responsible for more than 2000 miles of track, 6000 cars, and about 419 engines, including the "President," shown in the foreground.

Opposite, top: A railroad bridge in Tennessee's Racoon Range. Several railroad companies doubled their volume of business during the war.

Below: Federal engineers work on the construction of a bridge across the Tennessee River at Chattanooga in March 1864. By 1864 large sections of the Confederacy's railroad system had been destroyed. The Rebels destroyed Union railroads as well, but the Union army was, in many cases, able quickly to repair the damaged bridges and tracks. Sherman's army was especially proficient at repairing, as well as destroying, railroads. "The Atlanta campaign would simply have been quite impossible without the use of the railroads from Louisville to Nashville, from Nashville to Chattanooga, and from Chattanooga to Atlanta," he wrote in his memoirs.

Above: A prosperous farm in upstate New York. New machinery allowed women and children to keep farms productive even as men were going off to war. Meanwhile, demand for Northern crops increased during the war, not only because of the army's needs but because of crop failures in Europe. In the first two years of the conflict the North supplied Great Britain with about 40 percent of its wheat and flour.

Below: Women clerks leave work at the Treasury Department in Washington. During the war large numbers of women took jobs that previously had been filled by men.

Opposite: This Winslow Homer engraving shows a sewing circle, a common volunteer activity for women in both the North and the South.

Above, left: Slaves pick cotton. Before the war, Southerners believed England and France could not survive without "King Cotton." They were wrong. In 1861 the Europeans survived on an oversupply built up during the 1850s, and when the supply dwindled the following year, supplies from India and Egypt largely made up for the lack of imports from the Confederacy. Thus the Southern economy proved to be far weaker than Southerners had thought.

Below: New Yorkers riot for clothes in 1863. While the Northern economy generally flourished during the war, it had its weaknesses. The textiles industry suffered a sharp decline in productivity as a result of the limited cotton supply. Meanwhile, as wage increases lagged behind inflation many working class families faced new economic hardships.

Above, center: Rioters chase blacks through the streets of Manhattan in 1863.

Opposite, top right: New York rioters destroy brownstones on Lexington Avenue.

Opposite, bottom: Federal troops and rioters fire at each other in the streets of New York.

Above: Federal troops, called in shortly after returning from Gettysburg, disperse rioters with gunfire on Second Avenue.

Left: Southern women, living in Union-occupied territory, approach a Union commissary in hopes of getting food for their families.

Opposite, top: Southerners travel to the Union commissary to get supplies. As the war progressed food became increasingly scarce throughout the South. The basic problem was that Southern agriculture had concentrated so heavily on non-edible crops, but a complicating factor was that what food was available often spoiled while being slowly transported on overtaxed Southern railroads. The problem was, of course, most acute in cities under siege. A British visitor in Vicksburg when Grant had invested the city noted that the women and children had ''only the coarsest bacon to eat.'' Nonetheless, most Southerners preferred near-starvation to yielding to the Federals.

Opposite, bottom: A Union prisoner sketched this scene of an auction in Danville, North Carolina, where a five-dollar gold piece went for $150. Lacking cash to finance the war, the Confederacy, in 1861, began printing paper money without the revenues to back it up. The result was staggering inflation: by 1864, prices in the South were nearly 50 times what they had been in 1860. The alternative to this seemingly irresponsible policy would have been heavy taxation, but implementing such a policy was easier said than done. Southerners as a rule had an especially strong aversion to taxes, and the financial hardships brought about by the war only reinforced their feelings on the matter.

"War is cruelty, and you cannot refine it."
William Tecumseh Sherman, September 1984

During the first two years of the war the Union army had suffered from tentative leadership in the field and a lack of overall coordination of forces. By 1864, however, Lincoln had finally found a solution to these problems.

The President had for some time recognized the talents of Ulysses Grant, and in March 1864 he decided it was time to let the scruffy Ohioan take command of all Union armies. Grant immediately began drawing up a plan to integrate the disparate Federal forces into a comprehensive strategy: George Meade, who remained head of the Army of the Potomac after his victory at Gettysburg, was to concentrate on Lee in Virginia, while W.T. Sherman was to move against Joseph Johnston in Georgia. Meanwhile, auxiliary forces under Benjamin Butler, Franz Sigel and Nathaniel Banks would assist the two larger armies.

In part because Virginia was the more important theater, and perhaps because Grant trusted Sherman more than he trusted Meade, the new general-in-chief decided to remain in the East, where he could personally oversee the operation against Lee. On May 5 forces from the Army of the Potomac and the Army of Northern Virginia clashed in the Wilderness near Chancellorsville. When the battle ended two days later, some 28,000 men were dead, wounded or missing.

Although neither side emerged as the clear victor at the Battle of the Wilderness, the Confederates, in the end, had the edge, and the dispirited Yankees awaited Grant's orders to retreat. The next day, when Grant ordered the troops to march south, the Federals were exhilarated. The Yankees and Rebels clashed again near Spotsylvania, with no decisive results, and at various points to the south for the remainder of May. Then, after suffering a bitter defeat at Cold Harbor, the Union forces succeeded in eluding Lee and closed in on Petersburg, a rail center vital to Richmond's survival. The Rebels were able to come to Petersburg's defense barely in the nick of time. Both armies then settled in for a long siege.

Sherman, meanwhile, had been marching through Georgia and had gradually forced Johnston back toward Atlanta. On July 17, dismayed by Sherman's success, Jefferson Davis relieved Johnston of command, and replaced him with General John B. Hood. But Hood was no more successful than Johnston had been, and by the beginning of September the Confederates had surrendered Atlanta. Shortly after taking this important manufacturing and transportation center, Sherman ordered a civilian evacuation of the town to avoid the burden of looking after Georgians while trying to fight a war. Leaders in Atlanta vehemently protested the order as unusually cruel, but Sherman insisted it was necessary. Like Grant, he was committed to the idea that wars are fought against hostile peoples, not just against hostile armies. To win, an army needed to destroy resources and demoralize the supportive population, not simply force the retreat of troops on the battlefield.

In mid-November Sherman's army began its famous march to the sea. Over the next month the Yankee soldiers and a horde of stragglers inflicted more than $100 million-worth of damage in Georgia. By Sherman's own account, 80 percent of this was utter "waste and destruction." Much of the destruction was caused by soldiers and civilian vandals acting on their own accord: Sherman had in fact forbidden the wanton destruction of civilian property. But given his philosophy of war, such a result may have been inevitable.

Sherman's tactics drew little criticism in the North at the time: most Northerners were too weary of failure and too impressed with the drama of Sherman's march to begin questioning the morality of a successful general. As a result, the man who was viewed in the South as the very personification of evil was embraced by the North as a hero.

The fall of Atlanta not only boosted Northern morale, it raised Lincoln's political standing just in time to save his re-election bid against George B. McClellan. Lincoln had been losing ground earlier in the year when it had appeared that Grant and Sherman were stalled. Now that Sherman was making headway, Northern voters renewed their faith in Lincoln and re-elected him by a wide margin.

Previous pages: Union and Confederate troops clash outside Nashville, Tennessee.

Left: Rebel flag-of-truce ships pull in to Savannah in December 1864 to remove prisoners taken by Sherman.

Opposite top: Published shortly before the 1864 election, this Thomas Nast cartoon derides the idea of a negotiated peace with the Confederacy.

Opposite: In March 1864, near Dalton, Ga., Rebel troops mix it up in a big snowball fight.

GRANT MOVES ON RICHMOND

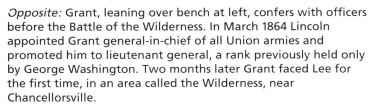

Opposite: Grant, leaning over bench at left, confers with officers before the Battle of the Wilderness. In March 1864 Lincoln appointed Grant general-in-chief of all Union armies and promoted him to lieutenant general, a rank previously held only by George Washington. Two months later Grant faced Lee for the first time, in an area called the Wilderness, near Chancellorsville.

Top: An artillery battery bogs down in the Wilderness mud. On May 4 Union troops, marching south, began crossing the Rapidan River. The next day they met the front lines of Lee's army coming in from the west. The dense woods severely limited visiblity, and the fighting became ever more chaotic as brush fires, sparked by the gunfire, began to spread.

Above, right: General G.K. Warren rallies his Maryland troops during the Battle of the Wilderness in this drawing by A.R. Waud. Despite violent fighting on the 5th the Yankees maintained their positions at the end of the day.

Above, left: Rebel infantry overrun a Union breastwork on Brock Road on May 6. On the morning of the 6th Winfield Scott Hancock's 2nd Corps drove the Confederates' right flank back about a mile before reinforcements under Longstreet stopped them. A counterattack then drove the Yankees back into the dense woods, where Longstreet was accidentally wounded by one of his own men. The Confederate advance bogged down temporarily after the loss of Longstreet, but the Rebels followed up with another assault at dusk, taking several hundred prisoners.

W. L Sheppard

Opposite, top: The Battle of the Wilderness. Despite devastating losses after two days of fighting, Grant refused to retreat. On the night of May 7 he ordered his army to resume marching south, toward Spotsylvania Courthouse. His aim was to take the fighting out of the deep woods where the power of Union artillery had been limited. Unfortunately for the Union, Lee anticipated the move. When Grant arrived, Rebels were waiting.

Opposite, bottom: A Currier & Ives version of the Battle of the Wilderness.

Above: Confederate soldiers await orders in the Wilderness. Between May 8 and May 11 the Yankees tried repeatedly to break through the Confederate line at Spotsylvania, but with little success. On May 12 Hancock's men managed to reach some of the Rebel trenches, but this success was tempered by vicious fighting nearby at a spot which came to be known as ''Bloody Angle.'' After hours of fighting, which resulted in thousands of casualties on each side, the Confederates still held the trenches.

Right: General Grant whittles in camp during a lull in the fighting at the Wilderness.

Left, top: Major General Wadsworth commands his men in the Wilderness.

Left, bottom: Lee rallies his troops at Spotsylvania.

Top: Union soldiers flee the brush fire in the Wilderness. As many as a hundred soldiers were burned to death by these fires.

Above: A line of Federals in the Wilderness on May 7. After two days of fighting in the Wilderness the Union had suffered 17,000 casualties, the Rebels about 11,000.

Above: General Hancock's 2nd Corps struggles to clear away small trees and brush along Brock Road. The Federals sustained heavy losses while holding this position.

Left: A renewed fighting spirit pervaded Grant's men when they marched from the Wilderness to Spotsylvania Courthouse. After the failures of the first two days many Union soldiers expected orders to retreat. When they realized Grant had no intention of backing off the men were jubilant that the previous day's fighting might still count for something.

Opposite, top: A Yankee charge near Spotsylvania Courthouse. While Grant's main force was attacking the Confederate line at Spotsylvania, Union cavalry leader Phil Sheridan was leading a raid behind the lines. In addition to destroying supplies and railroad tracks, the Yankee horsemen killed Confederate cavalry leader Jeb Stuart in a clash at Yellow Tavern.

Opposite, bottom: This drawing by Edwin Forbes shows the center of the Union position at Spotsylvania.

Opposite, top: Confederate prisoners captured at Spotsylvania.

Opposite, bottom: Jeb Stuart's final cavalry charge into battle at Yellow Tavern.

Above: After crossing the Rapidan, Grant writes a note to be telegraphed to Washington. On May 11 Grant had notified Washington that he would "fight it out on this line if it takes all summer."

Below: Union troops struggle to hold a captured trench during the fighting at Bloody Angle on May 12.

THE INVASION OF GEORGIA

Opposite: The Battle of Dug Gap, Ga., on May 8, 1864, one of the early clashes in Sherman's Atlanta campaign, in which 100,000 Union troops faced 50,000 Rebels under Joseph Johnston. The battles of the Atlanta campaign were, for the most part, not as fierce as those in Virginia during the same period because Sherman avoided frontal assaults through a series of flanking maneuvers. Johnston responded to Sherman's moves by repeatedly realigning his armies into strong defensive positions rather than attacking the Federals. Southerners sharply criticized Johnston for this defensive posture, and in July he was replaced by John B. Hood.

Right: Scenes from Sherman's march: Soldiers embark on an early morning foraging expedition (top) and return in the evening with their bounty. As Sherman moved toward Atlanta one of his key challenges was maintaining his supply lines. Eventually he loaded wagons with 20 days worth of supplies so his army would not be tied to the railroad.

Below: Sherman's army escorts captured Rebels from Jonesboro to Atlanta. On August 31, realizing Sherman's troops were closing in on Atlanta, Hood ordered an attack at Jonesboro. The assault failed, and Hood began evacuating Atlanta.

TENNESSEE

CHATTANOOGA

N. CAROLINA

4 May 1864
Sherman begins march south with:
Army of the Tennessee (McPherson), 24,000 troops
Army of the Cumberland (Thomas), 61,000 troops
Army of the Ohio (Schofield), 13,500 troops

RESACA

14 May
Sherman attacks, J. E. Johnston withdraws

ALABAMA

KINGSTON   CASSVILLE   **GEORGIA**

18/19 May
Johnston withdraws from defensive positions

Allatoona Pass

▲ *Kenesaw Mtn*

New Hope Church

27 June
Sherman repulsed with 3000 casualties

ATLANTA   Hood

JONESBORO

26 Aug
Union forces occupy Jonesboro, Confederates evacuate Atlanta

| MILES | 40 |
| KILOMETERS | 60 |

©Richard Natkiel, 1986

Chattahoochee   Peachtree Creek

Union Army
(Sherman)

Thomas   Schofield

Stewart   Hardee   **1500 hrs, 20 July**   McPherson

DECATUR

20 July
Confederate attack contained. Hood withdraws into Atlanta

1200 hrs, 22 July

Stewart   Cheatham   Cheatham

ATLANTA

Wheeler

Confederate Army
(Hood, replaces Johnston 17 July)

1200 hrs, 22 July   Hardee

22 July
McPherson killed during Hardee's attack, replaced by Howard

| MILES | 4 |
| KILOMETERS | 6 |

Previous pages: The Battle of Resaca and maps showing the positions of Yankee and Rebel armies during Sherman's March on Atlanta. In early May, Union troops under General James B. McPherson moved toward Resaca with the aim of destroying the railroad there. In the nick of time Johnston realized what was happening, moved his army to a new defensive position, and kept his supply line intact.

Above: The Battle of Jonesboro. In late August, Hood had ordered a cavalry raid, hoping to destroy Sherman's communications lines. Sherman began moving most of his army to the southwest, convincing Hood the Rebel raid had forced a Union retreat from Atlanta. When Sherman suddenly appeared at Jonesboro, Hood realized he had been outmaneuvered.

Below: An 1864 view of Atlanta, important to the Confederacy as a manufacturing center. With the Presidential election just two months away and anti-war sentiment gaining momentum, Sherman's capture of the city gave Lincoln a crucial political boost in his campaign.

Opposite, top: Fortifications in front of Atlanta in 1864. Grant told Sherman he had accomplished "the most gigantic undertaking given to any general in this war." Northern newspapers also praised Sherman's "brilliant strategic movement" and crowed over the fact that Hood had been, as they put it, "hoodwinked."

Below: The Battle of Kenesaw Mountain, the only serious setback suffered by Sherman's Army in the Atlanta campaign. On June 27, having driven Johnston's army back more than 70 miles in six weeks, Sherman ordered an assault on the Confederate center dug in near Kenesaw Mountain. Speaking of the Union charge in the face of withering fire, a Rebel recalled that the Yankees "seemed to walk up and take death as coolly as if they were automatic or wooden men." The Rebels drove Sherman's men off easily, inflicting some 3000 casualties in the process. The battle reinforced in Sherman's mind the conviction that frontal assaults on firmly entrenched enemy forces were to be avoided at all costs. He resumed his flanking strategy and slowly forced Johnston back to the outskirts of Atlanta.

Below: Soldiers in Sherman's army rip up a section of railroad in Atlanta. To maximize the damage, Sherman's men heated rails and tied them around trees. The twisted rails dotting the countryside became known as Sherman neckties.

Left: Confederate lines just north of the railroad leading to Atlanta.

Opposite, top: Southerners flee Sherman's army with what possessions they can carry. Because of the depredations committed by Sherman's army his campaign remains controversial to this day. ''War is cruelty and you cannot refine it,'' he told Atlanta's mayor, who had protested orders to evacuate the city. ''We don't want your Negroes or your horses or your houses or your lands. . . . But we do want, and will have, a just obedience to the laws of the United States . . .''

Opposite, top: Ruins of the Confederate enginehouse in Atlanta shortly after Sherman's conquest. Although Union soldiers were responsible for much of the city's destruction, Hood's army had also blown up factories and munitions to prevent their capture.

Opposite, bottom: A battery of the 5th U.S. Artillery takes up its position inside a captured Rebel fort near Atlanta. General Sherman is leaning against the wall (seventh from far right) in the background.

Right: A view of Nashville, Tennessee, where, in December 1864, the Union won a decisive victory.

Below, right: General Sherman. Some historians believe Sherman's Atlanta campaign was the most brilliant of the war because it accomplished so much with relatively few casualties. If this is true, it is ironic that Sherman is usually remembered not for the lives his strategy saved but for the destruction of property he wreaked in Georgia and the Carolinas. Yet Grant and Lincoln also believed in this strategy.

THE SIEGE OF PETERSBURG BEGINS

Capt Stevens battery on the 6th Corps skirmish line AR Waud

Opposite: Petersburg, Virginia. After the Battle of Cold Harbor, Grant moved toward Petersburg while sending out a cavalry screen to prevent Lee from learning of his plans. Building a 2200-foot pontoon bridge, Grant managed to get many of his troops across the James River before Lee had moved any of his. On June 15 the 18th Corps under General William F. Smith attacked Petersburg, forcing Rebels from the outermost works. Petersburg was virtually his, but Smith then faltered to wait for reinforcements. Smith's delay gave Lee enough time to get his own reinforcements into position, and Grant had no choice but to settle in for a siege.

Top: General Barlow and his men in front of Rebel works 12 miles from Richmond.

Second from top: Part of Grant's army crosses the Pamunkey River at Hanover Ferry, Virginia.

Above: Captain Stevens's battery on the 6th Corps skirmish line at Cold Harbor.

Right: Grant at Cold Harbor in June 1864.

The 18 Corps storming the fort on the left _____ ____ of the rebel line in front of
Petersburg on Wednesday evening June __
_____ ____ around the _____ column
June 15th 1864
E.F.

_____ N.Y. Heavy Arty — in Barlow's

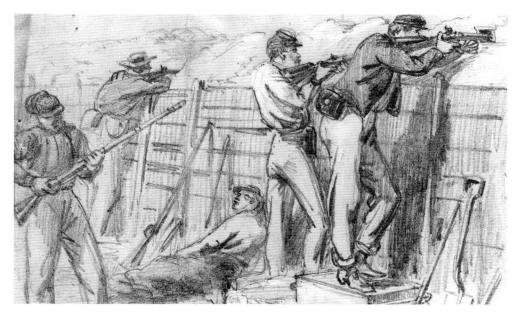

Aiming a mortar in Jackson's __

Previous pages: The Battle of Cold Harbor.

Opposite, top: An Edwin Forbes sketch made during General Smith's fumbled attack on Petersburg on June 15.

Opposite, center: Grant's army marches into battle at Cold Harbor.

Opposite, bottom left: Sharpshooters of the 18th Corps in the heat of battle at Cold Harbor. A Southern private recalled that Grant seemed ''determined to fight the decisive battle of the war. [He] massed his troops and rushed them on our works amidst a storm of shot and shell that it seemed no men could stand; but they were repulsed with great slaughter.''

Opposite, bottom right: Union troops prepare to fire a mortar during the battle of Cold Harbor.

Above: The 7th New York heavy artillery at Cold Harbor, June 3.

Opposite: The positions of Grant's army after it stalled at Petersburg. Settling in for the siege, some of Grant's men went to work reinforcing trenches and building mortar-proof shelters while others exchanged gunfire with the enemy.

Below: Union troops watch as a fellow soldier is hanged for desertion. The grueling conditions of the siege – the nonstop gunfire and hard labor under blistering heat and torrential rains – spurred desertions.

Above: Soldiers complete work on the pontoon bridge – the longest in history – across the James en route to Petersburg.

UNION   CONFEDERATE
TROOP DISPOSITIONS, 15 JUNE
18 JUNE

0700 Hrs, 15 June 1864
Smith attacks and breaks
through Confederate lines,
but waits for Hancock
who arrives in evening

Hancock

Smith

Union Army
(Grant)

Appomattox

PETERSBURG

Birney

1800 hrs, 16 June
Union attack
repulsed by
reinforced defenses

Beauregard

Burnside

Warren

Confederate Army
(Lee, arrives Petersburg
18 June)

0400 hrs
Grant's attack foiled by
Beauregard's withdrawal
to new defensive works

0   MILES   3

0   KILOMETERS   4

©Richard Natkiel, 1986

Below: Mathew Brady (in straw hat) observes a Union battery firing at Petersburg on June 21.

Left: A panoramic view of the fighting at Petersburg. Grant's efforts to break the siege were hampered by his army's lack of experience. In the campaign thus far he had lost 60 percent of his men.

Below, left: Johnson's Mill on the Appomattox River near Petersburg.

Right: Union and Confederate cavalry clash at Trevilian Station on June 12.

Scene of the Explosion. Saturday July 30th. A.R. Waud

Explosion at City Point A.R. Waud

Opposite, top: The Battle of the Crater. Toward the end of July a Union colonel named Henry Pleasants came up with a seemingly crazy yet ingenious plan. To break through Rebel defenses at Petersburg he would dig a mine shaft under enemy lines and blow the fortifications wide open with massive amounts of gunpowder. Amazingly, the plan worked – or at least the part of it for which Pleasants was responsible. On July 30 hundreds of Rebels were blasted from their trenches, but the Federals failed to follow through in an organized fashion. Many of them charged into the crater that had been created by the explosion and became easy targets after the Rebels had recovered from the surprise. Thus the Union lost yet another golden opportunity.

Opposite, bottom left: A Union battery digs a trench during the grim siege of Petersburg.

Opposite, bottom right: Jubal Early. In the beginning of July, Early led his Confederate cavalry across the Potomac toward Washington in hopes of relieving pressure on Richmond. By July 11 he had made it to the outskirts of the capital, but he was obliged to call off the raid after Union reinforcements arrived. Before leaving, however, he managed to burn the home of the Postmaster General and take more than $200,000 from two Maryland cities. He then set fire to a third city after its residents refused to pay the levy he demanded. Upon learning of Early's exploits Grant ordered Philip Sheridan to "follow him to the death" and to destroy crops throughout the Shenandoah Valley in the process.

Top: The Battle of Petersburg.

Above: Part of the railroad at City Point, Virginia, is blown up on August 9. Drawing by A.R. Waud.

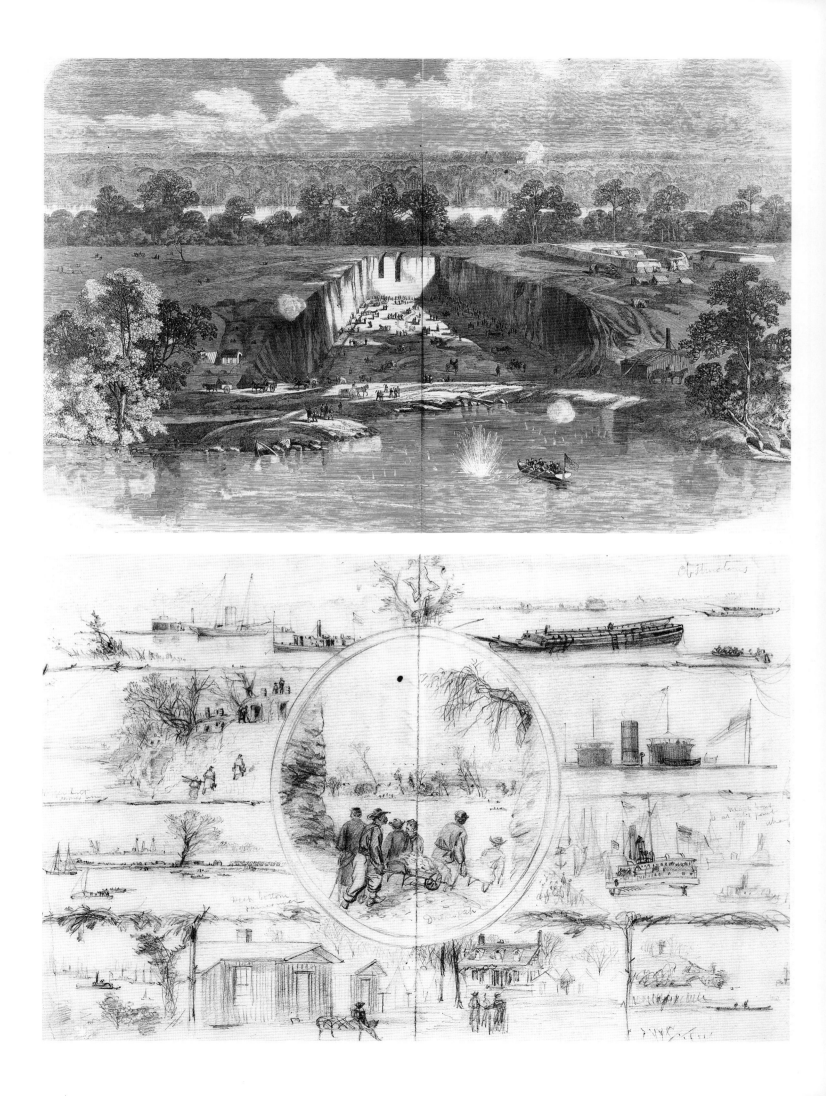

Opposite, top: Union soldiers under General Butler work on the Dutch Gap Canal across the Virginia peninsula.

Opposite, bottom: This composite of sketches by A.R. Waud depicts scenes on the James River during the Petersburg campaign. At center, men work on the Dutch Gap Canal.

Above, left: A Union infantryman peers out of his "bombproof" rifle pit at Petersburg.

Above, right: Guns and mantelets along the Union lines during the siege of Petersburg.

Right: An artillery wagon at Union headquarters at Petersburg.

Below: A view from inside the partially completed Dutch Gap Canal, which would prove militarily useless.

Below: Defenses at Petersburg. Throughout the summer and fall Grant continued to stretch his line westward, forcing Lee to do the same until the Rebel defenses were dangerously thin. After a harsh winter, Petersburg fell in the spring.

Opposite, left: Bombproof quarters at the Union's Fort Sedgwick, later nicknamed "Fort Hell."

Opposite, right: Blacksmiths in the Army of the Potomac work on horseshoes during the siege of Petersburg.

Right: Interior of a fort near Petersburg. On September 29 Grant ordered attacks on Forts Harrison and Gilmore on the Petersburg line. General George Stannard captured Harrison, but the Yankees failed to take Gilmore.

242

Left: Entrenchments abandoned by the Confederates early in the siege of Petersburg.

Below: Union soldiers await Grant's orders in the trenches near Petersburg in 1865.

Opposite: Major General Philip Sheridan. At the outset of the war, Sheridan was a lieutenant who showed little promise. He had once been suspended from West Point for assaulting another student and, later, came close to being court-martialed. In November 1863, however, Sheridan's impressive performance at Missionary Ridge convinced Grant that the one-time trouble-maker deserved to play a greater role in the war. The following April, Grant appointed Sheridan cavalry commander of the Army of the Potomac and in August gave him overall command of the Army of the Shenandoah.

Above: Sheridan's army marches into the Shenandoah Valley. On September 19 Sheridan attacked Jubal Early's Confederate troops near Winchester, crushing the enemy's left flank. The Confederate center gave way more slowly, but by the 22nd Sheridan had driven the Rebel forces back 80 miles to Brown's Gap. Having delivered a stunning blow to the enemy in battle, Sheridan proceeded to further weaken them by destroying the area's crops and livestock.

Below: Sheridan (center) and his staff.

Opposite, top: Sheridan gathers some roadside intelligence. Behind him is his flamboyant subordinate, George Armstrong Custer.

Opposite, bottom: The Union begins what would be its decisive charge at the stone wall in the Battle of Winchester on September 19, 1864.

Top, right: Mosby's Rangers rendezvous in the Blue Ridge Mountains. John Singleton Mosby served as a private in the Virginia cavalry and subsequently as a lieutenant under Jeb Stuart. In January 1863 the Confederacy gave him permission to organize his own band of "irregulars" or guerrillas. During the second valley campaign Mosby's gang disrupted communication and supply lines while terrorizing both civilians and soldiers on the periphery of Sheridan's army. These guerrilla actions hampered Sheridan by diverting him from his main objective.

Center, right: George Crook's corps in the Battle of Winchester.

Below: Sheridan's troops advance after the Battle of Winchester in September.

Blue ground white star

men exceedingly rough

Opposite, top: General Custer, in Washington on October 23, presents flags captured during the last battle of the Valley campaign. Sheridan's victories in the valley gave Lincoln yet another crucial pre-election boost.

Opposite, bottom: Sheridan's ride at Cedar Creek on October 19, one of the most dramatic moments of the war. By the middle of October, Early had rebuilt much of his army, and on October 18 he launched a surprise attack on the Federals near Cedar Creek. Sheridan was in Winchester, nearly 20 miles away, but upon hearing the distant gunfire he galloped off toward the battlefield. When he arrived he rallied his nearly beaten troops and launched a powerful counterattack, driving the Rebels back over the ground they had gained and then some.

Above: Sheridan's ride, which has become legendary. The ride itself was the subject of a poem by Thomas Buchanan Read. His horse, Rienzi, was later stuffed and now stands in the Smithsonian Institution.

Right: A full-bearded Sheridan portrayed by Thomas Nast.

Opposite: Rear Admiral Raphael Semmes, commander of the Confederate raider *Alabama.* Attacks by the *Alabama* cost the Union over $6.5 million.

Top: The crew of USS *Kearsarge* prepares to fire the ship's 11-inch forward pivot-gun. In June 1864 the *Kearsarge* cornered the *Alabama* in the harbor of Cherbourg, France. Confederate Captain Semmes then challenged the captain of the Union sloop to a battle on open water, and the Union commander accepted.

Above: Acting Master Eben M. Stoddard, left, and Chief Engineer William H. Cushman, on the *Kearsarge* in June 1864.

Right: Captain John A. Winslow, third from left, and officers aboard the *Kearsarge* after the sinking of the *Alabama.*

also threatened Farragut's ships. Before the morning was out one of the ironclads had been sunk. Undaunted, Farragut's fleet pressed ahead.

Left: The Battle of Mobile Bay. Shortly after the sinking of the Union ship, a Confederate ironclad, the *Tennessee*, joined the battle. Taking advantage of the ironclad's poor maneuverability, three Union vessels began ramming from all sides. An hour later the captain of the *Tennessee* surrendered, and the Union quickly took control of Mobile Bay.

Center: Rear Admiral David G. Farragut, who is reported to have yelled "Damn the torpedoes! Full speed ahead!" after the sinking of the Union ironclad *Tecumseh* in Mobile Bay. Farragut's naval career began under David Porter during the War of 1812. Though not yet in his teens at the time, Farragut was taken prisoner by the British. Half a century later he made his daring run past Confederate forts on the Mississippi River below New Orleans and established his reputation as one of the Union's most effective commanders.

Below: The Battle of Mobile Bay, a line drawing by eyewitness George S. Waterman.

Opposite, bottom: The "Alabama."

Opposite, top: The Battle of Mobile Bay. In August 1864 Rear Admiral David G. Farragut, the conqueror of New Orleans, moved to close down one of the few ports still under Confederate control. On August 5 four Union ironclads and 14 wooden ships entered Mobile Bay in Alabama. The Union fleet immediately drew heavy fire from Confederate gunboats and nearby forts, and "moored torpedoes" (mines)

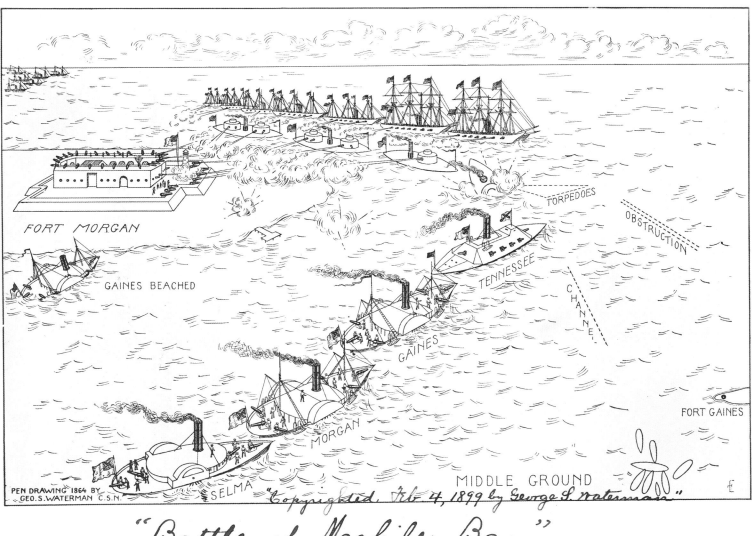

PEN DRAWING 1864 BY GEO. S. WATERMAN C.S.N.

FORT MORGAN

GAINES BEACHED

TENNESSEE

TORPEDOES

OBSTRUCTION

CHANNEL

GAINES

FORT GAINES

MORGAN

SELMA

MIDDLE GROUND

"Copyrighted, Feb. 4, 1899 by George S. Waterman"

"Battle of Mobile Bay"

THE CAROLINAS CAMPAIGN

Opposite: Union General Hugh J. Kilpatrick and his troops repulse a Rebel attack at Waynesboro, Georgia, on December 4. Kilpatrick had been assigned to guard railroad wrecking crews.

Above, left: Sherman's headquarters in Pine Woods.

Above, right: Sherman reviews Kilpatrick's division at Marietta, Georgia, on November 13. Three days later Sherman's army of 62,000 began its infamous march to Savannah and the sea in two diverging columns. Sherman promised to "make Georgia howl. . . . We cannot change the hearts of these people of the South," he wrote, "but we can make . . . them so sick of war that generations [will] pass away before they again appeal to it." By the time they reached Savannah, five weeks later, his men had inflicted roughly $100 million-worth of property damage.

Below: Sherman's army marches through South Carolina on February 1, 1865.

Above, left: Confederates burn a Navy vessel in dry dock at Savannah Navy yard on December 21, 1864. On December 17, as Sherman closed in on Savannah, he had sent Confederate General William J. Hardee a message demanding surrender of the city. Hardee refused. Three days later Hardee realized he could not hold the city and began to move his Rebel troops northward. Before leaving they burned ships to prevent them from falling into the hands of the Union.

Above, right: A caricature of Sherman as Santa Claus, placing the city of Savannah in Uncle Sam's Christmas stocking. The engraving, which appeared in *Frank Leslie's Illustrated*

Newspaper shortly after the city fell, was inspired by Sherman's own dispatch to Lincoln: ''I beg to present you, as a Christmas gift, the city of Savannah, with 150 heavy guns and plenty of ammunition. . . .''

Below: Confederate soldiers evacuate Savannah on December 21. After leaving Savannah, Hardee headed toward South Carolina, where he hoped to pull together reinforcements.

Opposite, top: Sherman's route through Georgia and the Carolinas, culminating in Johnston's surrender to Sherman in Raleigh on April 14.

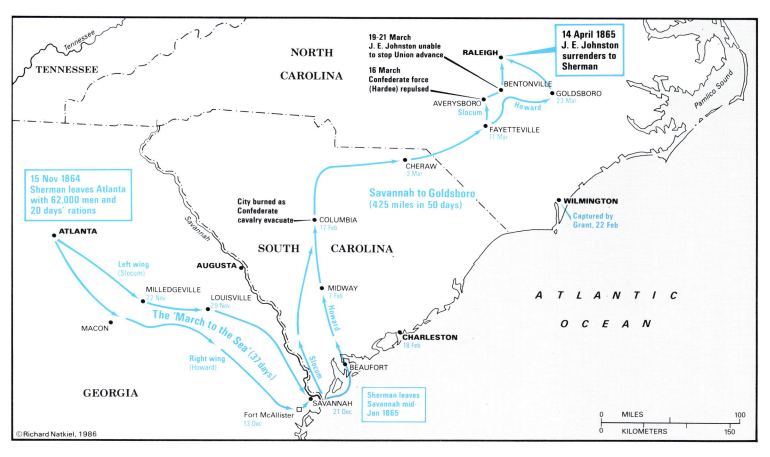

14 April 1865
J. E. Johnston surrenders to Sherman

19-21 March
J. E. Johnston unable
to stop Union advance

NORTH
CAROLINA

RALEIGH

16 March
Confederate force
(Hardee) repulsed

BENTONVILLE

GOLDSBORO
23 Mar

AVERYSBORO

Howard

Slocum

FAYETTEVILLE
11 Mar

TENNESSEE

Tennessee

CHERAW
3 Mar

Savannah to Goldsboro
(425 miles in 50 days)

WILMINGTON

15 Nov 1864
Sherman leaves Atlanta
with 62,000 men and
20 days' rations

City burned as
Confederate
cavalry evacuate

COLUMBIA
17 Feb

Captured by
Grant, 22 Feb

ATLANTA

Savannah

SOUTH   CAROLINA

Left wing
(Slocum)

AUGUSTA

MILLEDGEVILLE
22 Nov

LOUISVILLE
29 Nov

MIDWAY
7 Feb

ATLANTIC

MACON

The 'March to the Sea' (37 days)

Howard

OCEAN

Right wing
(Howard)

Slocum

CHARLESTON
18 Feb

GEORGIA

BEAUFORT

SAVANNAH
21 Dec

Sherman leaves
Savannah mid-
Jan 1865

Fort McAllister
13 Dec

Pamlico Sound

©Richard Natkiel, 1986

0   MILES   100
0   KILOMETERS   150

Right: Sherman's army marches into Columbia, South Carolina, on February 17, 1865. In early January, Sherman had transferred part of his army from Savannah to Beaufort, South Carolina. Heavy rains throughout the latter part of January interrupted further movement, but on February 1 the Carolinas campaign began in earnest. Once again, to confuse the Rebels as to his true direction, Sherman divided his army, sending the right wing toward Charleston and the left toward Augusta. When the Rebels moved to reinforce both cities, Sherman cut the railroad link between them and moved on to Columbia.

Opposite, top: Residents of Charleston, South Carolina, run for cover as a shell bursts overhead. Cut off from the rest of the state by Sherman's army and besieged by Union forces off the coast, Charleston surrendered on February 18.

Opposite, bottom: A Brady photograph of Charleston.

Above: Residents of Charleston flee as the city is bombarded.

260

Left: Sherman, as he appeared in 1888.

Bottom: Soldiers gather on the outskirts of Columbia as the city burns. The burning of Columbia is often cited as an example of Sherman's cruelty, but the fires appear to have been set by various hands: Confederate troops seeking to destroy cotton before the Union could seize it, drunken civilians engaged in looting, and soon-to-be-freed slaves.

Opposite, bottom: A lone resident passes through the ruined South Carolina capital.

Opposite, top left: Victorious troops raise the American flag over the Capitol building at Columbia on February 17.

Opposite, top right: General Joseph E. Johnston. On February 6 Lee had become general-in-chief of all Confederate armies. Shortly thereafter he reappointed Johnston to his old command in a final attempt to stop Sherman.

Below: Sherman and Johnston meet to discuss terms of Confederate surrender. For two months after the fall of Columbia, Sherman's and Johnston's armies had skirmished. Finally, on April 14, Johnston requested a cease-fire.

1865

"There is nothing left to do but to go and see General Grant, and I would rather die a thousand deaths."

Robert E. Lee, April 1865

Sherman's march through Georgia in the latter part of 1864 had destroyed more than crops and buildings — it had cracked the Southern will to fight.

Amazingly, the Rebels' fighting spirit had remained high through much of 1864, despite incredible hardships in the field and grave worries about the welfare of families back home. Cold weather severely aggravated these hardships, however, bringing many soldiers to the breaking point. News of Sherman's success seemed to confirm that the Confederate cause was hopeless.

By March, Confederate leaders were so desperate that they decided to do the unthinkable: arm slaves and hope that they would fight for the South. Many Southerners opposed the move, for obvious reasons. But Lee supported the proposal, and on March 13 the Confederate Congress passed a bill allowing for the enlistment of blacks.

While Southerners were beginning to recognize, if only implicitly, the death of their beloved institution, Northerners were putting the last nails in its coffin. In January 1865 the Federal Congress passed the 13th Amendment, which prohibited slavery unconditionally. The amendment would not be fully ratified until December, as a condition of Reconstruction, but the message was clear all over the land: slavery was a thing of the past.

Having driven the Confederate army to the brink of destruction, the Federals now waited for the right opportunity to finish their enemies off. The opportunity finally presented itself in late March when Lee made one last attempt to hit Grant's flank and break the siege at Petersburg. The ensuing battle did not go well for the Rebels, and within a matter of hours they had suffered nearly 5000 casualties.

Pressing his advantage, Grant went on the offensive and did not let up. By April 2 the Confederates had abandoned Richmond as well as Petersburg, and a week later Lee's army was trapped near Appomattox Courthouse.

On April 9 the two generals met to discuss terms of surrender. Grant proposed a parole for Lee's entire army and allowed the beaten Rebels to keep their sidearms and horses. He also offered rations for the starving Southerners. Many years later Grant recalled how saddened he had been at Lee's downfall. Grant's melancholy was nothing compared with the grief that would soon pervade the nation when an even greater hero fell, for five days after Lee's surrender Lincoln was assassinated. Thus a war that had been laced with cruel ironies ended on a note more ironic than any other: Northerners were left to celebrate the salvation of the Union while mourning the death of the man who had been most responsible for preserving it.

Previous pages: The Battle of Opequan Creek at Winchester, Va., – the third battle to be fought in the area – ended in a decisive victory for the Union.

Opposite: Fought on March 20, 1865, the Battle of Bentonville was virtually CSA General J.E. Johnston's last effort to stem the tide of Sherman's advance into North Carolina.

Right: A Thomas Nast sketch of the surrender at Appomattox.

Below: In this engraving of the surrender negotiations in the McLean house in Appomattox Courthouse a solitary Lee faces Grant and a phalanx of Union generals.

THE SURRENDER OF GEN LEE AND HIS ARMY TO LIEUT. GEN GRANT

HONOR THE ILLUSTRIOUS DEAD.
AND HEARTILY SYMPATHIZE WITH THE SUFFERINGS
OF OUR GALLANT
HEROES AND THEIR FAMILIES.

THE APPOMATTOX CAMPAIGN

Above: Union artillery charge into battle at Petersburg. On March 25 Lee ordered one last attack on Union forces near Petersburg.

Top: Federals take Fort Gregg, the last Confederate stronghold at Petersburg, on April 2, 1865. It was one of the war's bloodiest clashes. On April 1 Sheridan had delivered a crushing blow to the Rebels at a junction called Five Forks. Grant capitalized on this victory with an all-out assault on the Petersburg line the following day. The Federals were again victorious, but the assault was not as successful as Grant had hoped: the Union suffered 4000 casualties, and Lee's army had once more escaped.

Right: Union troops march into the trenches at Richmond. As Rebels retreated across the Appomattox River, the Confederacy abandoned its capital.

Opposite: Richmond residents gather in Capitol Square after the fall of the city.

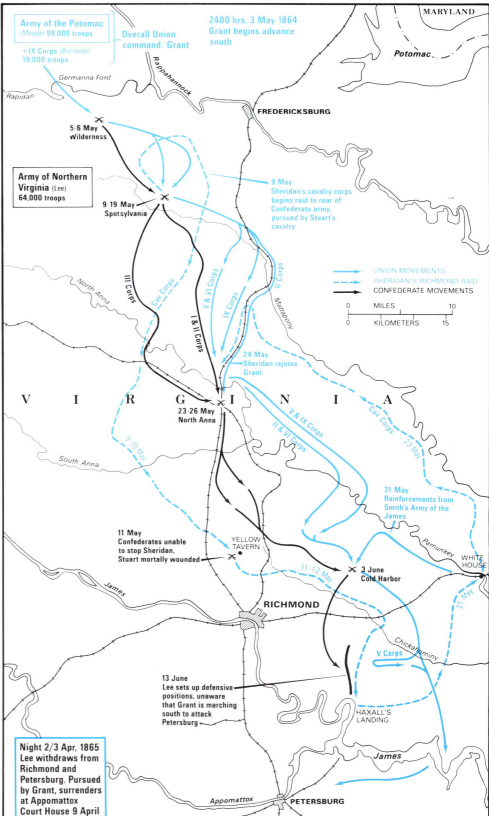

The map contains the following labels:

MARYLAND

Potomac

Army of the Potomac (Meade) 99,000 troops

Overall Union command: Grant

+ IX Corps (Burnside) 19,000 troops

2400 hrs, 3 May 1864 Grant begins advance south

Germanna Ford

Rappahannock

Rapidan

FREDERICKSBURG

5-6 May Wilderness

Army of Northern Virginia (Lee) 64,000 troops

9 May Sheridan's cavalry corps begins raid to rear of Confederate army, pursued by Stuart's cavalry

9-19 May Spotsylvania

III Corps

Cav Corps

V & VI Corps

IX Corps

I & II Corps

II Corps

Mattaponi

UNION MOVEMENTS
SHERIDAN'S RICHMOND RAID
CONFEDERATE MOVEMENTS

MILES 0 — 10
KILOMETERS 0 — 15

24 May Sheridan rejoins Grant

V I R G I N I A

North Anna

23-26 May North Anna

V & IX Corps

II & VI Corps

Cav Corps 23 May

South Anna

9-10 May

31 May Reinforcements from Smith's Army of the James

11 May Confederates unable to stop Sheridan, Stuart mortally wounded

YELLOW TAVERN

11-12 May

3 June Cold Harbor

Pamunkey

WHITE HOUSE

James

RICHMOND

21 May

Chickahominy

V Corps

13 June Lee sets up defensive positions, unaware that Grant is marching south to attack Petersburg

HAXALL'S LANDING

James

Night 2/3 Apr, 1865 Lee withdraws from Richmond and Petersburg. Pursued by Grant, surrenders at Appomattox Court House 9 April

Appomattox

PETERSBURG

©Richard Natkiel, 1986

Opposite, top left: Grant, as he appeared in 1865. After finally defeating Lee, Grant was far from jubilant. He simply could not bring himself to celebrate ''the downfall of a foe who had fought so long and valiantly and had suffered so much for a cause, though that cause was . . . one of the worst for which a people ever fought.''

Top, Center: Richmond continues to burn after falling into Union hands. As they had done before when abandoning other cities, the retreating Rebels had put the torch to everything of military value in Richmond before evacuating it. By the time Union troops extinguished the fires much of the city had been destroyed.

Opposite, bottom: The ruins of Richmond in 1865.

Above, right: Grant's advance on Richmond. As Richmond burned, Sheridan's cavalry and two Union infantry corps raced after Lee's retreating army. By April 9 the Rebels were trapped.

Above, left: Robert E. Lee in 1865.

Opposite, top: Mourning Confederate women pass through the ruins of Richmond.

Opposite, bottom: Ruins of Mayo's Railroad Bridge, which was destroyed by Rebel cavalry shortly before the fall of Richmond.

Right: A few building facades stand amidst the rubble of a Richmond street.

Below, right: An engraving for the cover of a pamphlet celebrating the fall of Richmond.

Opposite, top: Former slaves in Richmond after the Confederate evacuation.

Opposite, bottom: The McClean house at Appomattox Courthouse where Grant met Lee to discuss terms of surrender. Four years earlier McClean's house near Bull Run had been used as a Rebel headquarters. He had come to Appomattox in hopes of escaping the war.

Above: The Battle of Five Forks, Virginia, where 5000 Rebels fell in a clash with Sheridan's cavalry and the 5th Corps. The Federals lost 1000 men in the battle.

Below, left: Union and Confederate positions during the Battle of Five Forks.

Below, right: The Union army marches through Richmond.

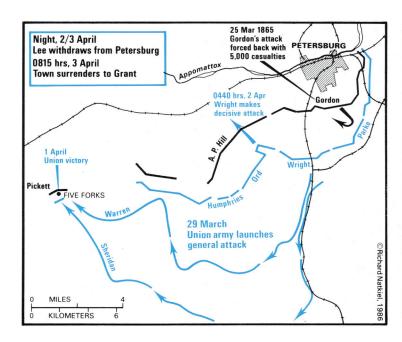

Night, 2/3 April
Lee withdraws from Petersburg
0815 hrs, 3 April
Town surrenders to Grant

25 Mar 1865
Gordon's attack forced back with 5,000 casualties

PETERSBURG

Appomattox

Gordon

0440 hrs, 2 Apr
Wright makes decisive attack

A. P. Hill

Parke

Wright

Ord

1 April
Union victory

Pickett

FIVE FORKS

Humphries

Warren

29 March
Union army launches general attack

Sheridan

0   MILES   4
0   KILOMETERS   6

©Richard Natkiel, 1986

Top, left: Ewell's troops surrender on April 6. The fleeing Rebels had sealed their fate after they accidentally split into two segments. As a result of the error, the Federals overwhelmed them and captured nearly a third of Lee's army, losing about 1200 men in the process.

Above: The message Lee sent to Grant requesting a meeting to discuss terms of surrender. Lee had said that he "would rather die a thousand deaths" than meet with Grant, but he realized that defeat was inevitable and that further attempts to postpone it would only cause more suffering for the people of Virginia.

Left, center: Union General George A. Custer receives the flag of truce on April 8.

Bottom, left: Confederate soldiers bid a tearful farewell to their defeated leader. One witness recalled how battle-hardened Rebels "threw themselves on the ground . . . and wept like children."

Opposite: Correspondence between Grant and Stanton, and between Grant and Lee, regarding the surrender. Grant agreed to a general parole for Lee's men.

SURRENDER OF Gen. LEE,

AND THE ARMY OF NORTHERN VIRGINIA

WAR DEPARTMENT, APRIL 9, 1865.

GENERAL STEVENSON:

This Department has just received the official report of the surrender of General Lee and his army to Lieut. General Grant, on the terms proposed by General Grant. Details will be given as speedily as possible.   E. M. STANTON.

HEADQUARTERS ARMIES OF THE UNITED STATES,

4:30, P. M., April 9, 1865.

To E. M. STANTON, Secretary of War.

General Lee surrendered the Army of Northern Virginia, this afternoon, upon terms proposed by myself. The accompanying additiona correspondence will show the conditions fully.   U. S. GRANT, Lieutenant General.

GENERAL,   APRIL 9, 1865.

I received your note of this morning on the picket line, where I had come to meet you and ascertain definitely what terms were embraced in your proposal of yesterday with reference to the surrender of this army. I now request an interview in accordance with the offer contained in your letter of yesterday, for that purpose.

Very respectfully, your obedient servant,

To Lt. Gen. U. S. GRANT, Comd'g U. S. Armies.   R. E. LEE, General.

General R. E. LEE, Com'dg C. S. Armies.   April 9, 1865.

Your note of this date is but this moment (11.50, A. M.) received,   in consequence of my having passed from the Richmond and Lynchburg road to the Farmville and Lynchburg road.   I am, at this time, waiting about four miles west of Waller's Church, and will push forward to the front for the purpose of meeting you. Notice sent to me on this road, where you wish the interview to take place, will meet me.   Very respectfully, your obedient servant,   U. S. GRANT, Lieut. Genneral

APPOMATTOX COURT HOUSE, April 9, 1865.

General R. E. LEE, Commanding C. S. A.

In accordance with the substance of my letter through you, of the 8th inst., I propose to receive the surrender of the Army of Northern Virginia, on the following terms, to wit : Rolls of all officers and men, to be made in duplicate, one copy to be given to an officer designated by me, the other to be retained by such officer or officers as you may designate. The officers to give their individual parole not to take arms against the Government of the United States, until properly exchanged ; and each Company or Regimental Commander sign a parole for the men of their command. The Arms, Artillery and public property to be parked and stacked, and turned over to the officers appointed by me to receive them. This will not embrace the side-arms of the officers, nor their private horses or baggage· This done, each officer and man will be allowed to return to their homes, not to be disturbed by United States authority so long as they observe their parole and the laws in force where they may reside.   Very respectfully, your obedient servant,   U. S. GRANT, Lieut. General.

HEADQUARTERS ARMY OF NORTHERN VIRGINIA,

April 9, 1865.

To Lieut. General U. S. GRANT, Commanding.

General —I have received your letter of this date, containing the terms of surrender of the Army of Northern Virginia, as proposed by you ; as they are substantially the same as those expressed in your letter of 8th inst., they are accepted.   I will proceed to designate the proper officer to carry the stipulations into effect.   Very respectfully, your obedient servant,   R. E. LEE, General.

Above, left: Union soldiers share rations with their defeated enemies at Appomattox. After the surrender Grant urged his men not to celebrate: ''The war is over,'' he said. ''The Rebels are our countrymen again.''

Above, right: Starving Rebel soldiers wait in line as a Union soldier hands out food. During Grant's meeting with Lee the Union general offered 25,000 rations for the defeated army. ''This will have the best possible effect on my men,'' Lee said. ''It will be very gratifying and do much toward conciliating our people.''

Below: James Bennett's house, where Joseph E. Johnston surrendered to William Tecumseh Sherman.

Opposite: Lee's farewell address. ''I have done the best I could for you,'' Lee told his men. ''Go home now, and if you make as good citizens as you have soldiers, you will do well, and I shall always be proud of you. Goodbye and God bless you all.''

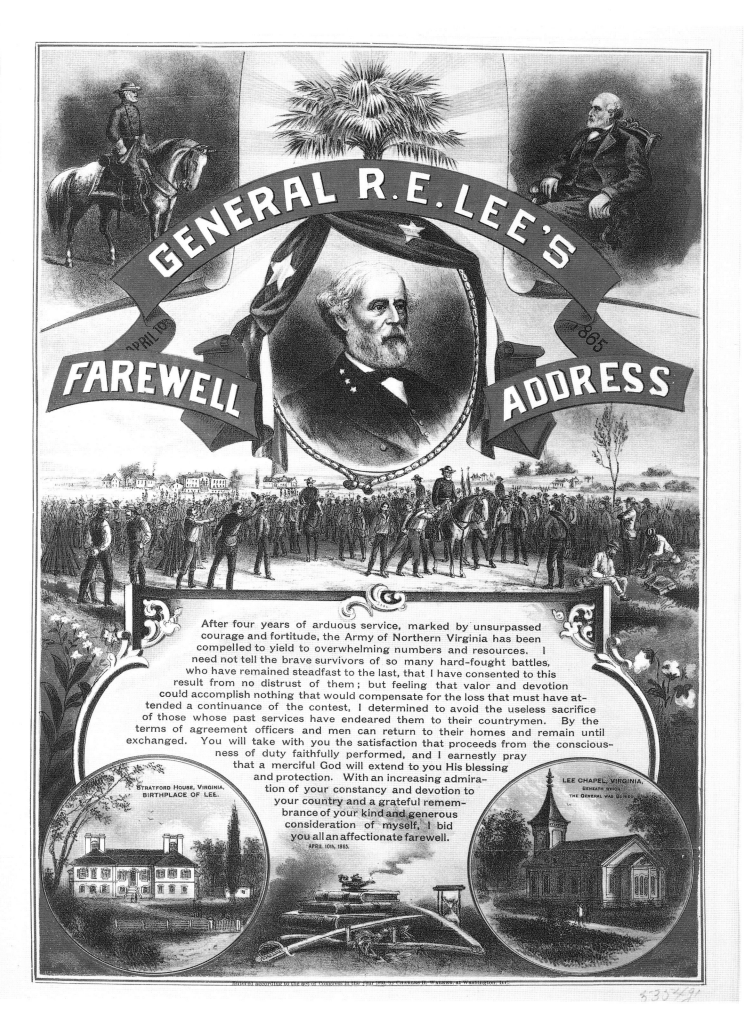

GENERAL R.E. LEE'S
FAREWELL ADDRESS

APRIL 10th 1865

STRATFORD HOUSE, VIRGINIA, BIRTHPLACE OF LEE.

LEE CHAPEL, VIRGINIA, BENEATH WHICH THE GENERAL WAS BURIED.

After four years of arduous service, marked by unsurpassed courage and fortitude, the Army of Northern Virginia has been compelled to yield to overwhelming numbers and resources. I need not tell the brave survivors of so many hard-fought battles, who have remained steadfast to the last, that I have consented to this result from no distrust of them; but feeling that valor and devotion could accomplish nothing that would compensate for the loss that must have attended a continuance of the contest, I determined to avoid the useless sacrifice of those whose past services have endeared them to their countrymen. By the terms of agreement officers and men can return to their homes and remain until exchanged. You will take with you the satisfaction that proceeds from the consciousness of duty faithfully performed, and I earnestly pray that a merciful God will extend to you His blessing and protection. With an increasing admiration of your constancy and devotion to your country and a grateful remembrance of your kind and generous consideration of myself, I bid you all an affectionate farewell.

APRIL 10th, 1865.

FAMOUS UNION COMMANDERS OF THE CIVIL WAR, 1861-'65.

GEN. GEO. H. THOMAS.   GEN. PHILIP KEARNEY.   GEN. A. E. BURNSIDE.   GEN. JOSEPH HOOKER.   GEN. JOHN A. LOGAN.   GEN. GEO. G. MEADE.   GEN. GEO. B. McCLELLAN.

ADMIRAL DAVID G. FARRAGUT.   GEN. JOHN POPE.   GEN. PHILIP H. SHERIDAN.   GEN. U. S. GRANT.   GEN. W. T. SHERMAN.   GEN. W. S. ROSECRANS.   GEN. DANIEL E. SICKLES.

GEN. BENJAMIN F. BUTLER.   GEN. WINFIELD S. HANCOCK.   GEN. JOHN SEDGWICK.   ADMIRAL DAVID D. PORTER.

Published by the Sherman Publishing Co. New York.   Copyrighted 1884, by the Sherman Publishing Co. New York.

This, and a Companion Engraving, representing TWENTY (20) FAMOUS CONFEDERATE COMMANDERS, given as PREMIUMS to Subscribers to the Book "The Pictorial Battles of the Civil War," Published by the Sherman Publishing Co., New York.

Opposite, top: Prominent Union and Confederate generals and statesmen, with Lee and Grant in the center.

Opposite, bottom: Top Union commanders. Grant, Sherman, Thomas and Sheridan were among the Union's most able leaders. Several others shared two fatal flaws: unwillingness to press their numerical superiority and inability to capitalize on victories.

Right: Robert E. Lee, shortly after Appomattox.

Below: The Grand Review of the Union army was held in the rejoined nation's capital on May 23, 1865.

Above: A pass for a paroled prisoner of the Army of Northern Virginia, signed by General W.N. Pendleton.

THE LAST DAYS OF LINCOLN

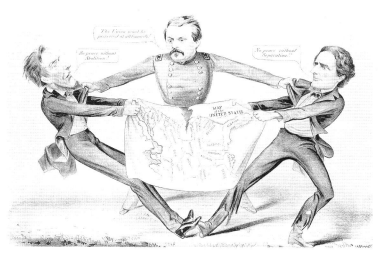

Opposite: Abraham Lincoln in February 1864.

Above, left: This Currier & Ives lithograph portrays McClellan, center, as the moderate candidate for President in 1864, while Lincoln is depicted as no less an extremist than Davis.

Above, right: This allegorical sketch by Thomas Nast, published in *Harper's* on December 31, 1864, features the essential elements of

Lincoln's Reconstruction policy. Lincoln stands at the doorway of a great banquet hall in which representatives of loyal states are seated and welcomes Jefferson Davis, Robert E. Lee and other former Rebels.

Below: Soldiers in the Army of the Potomac vote in the national Presidential election of 1864.

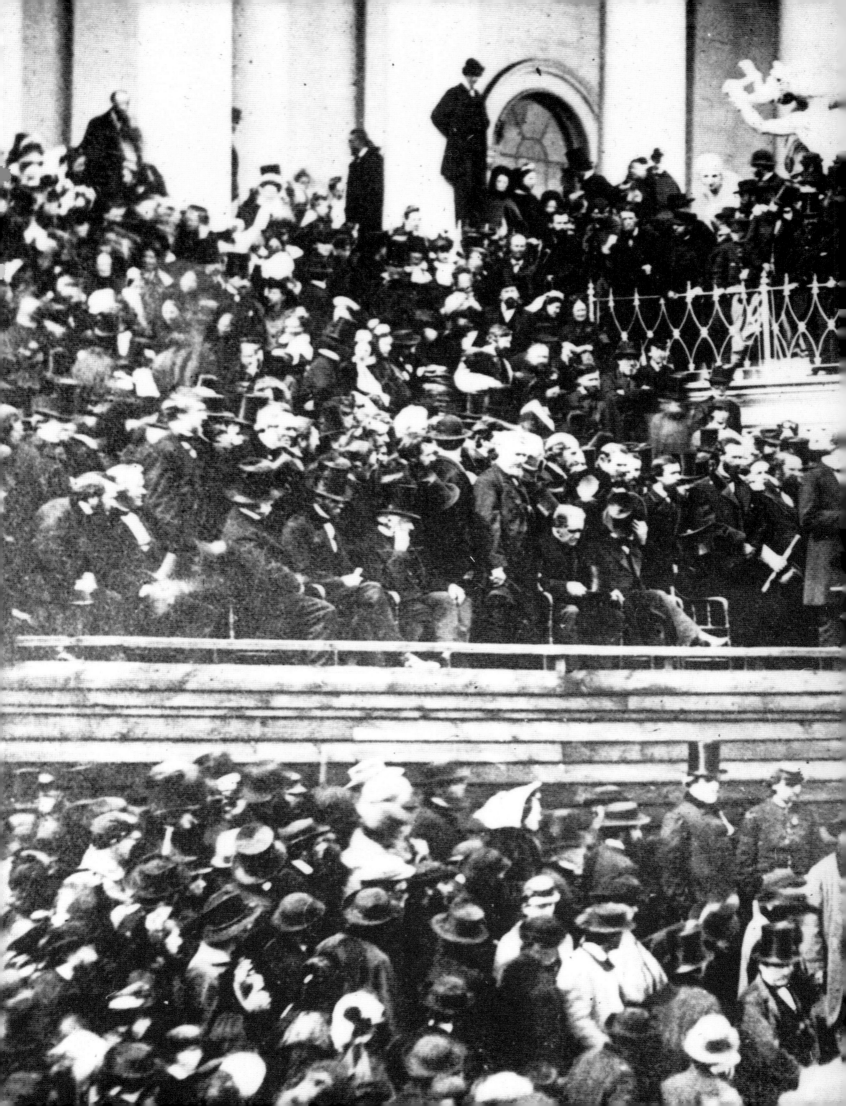

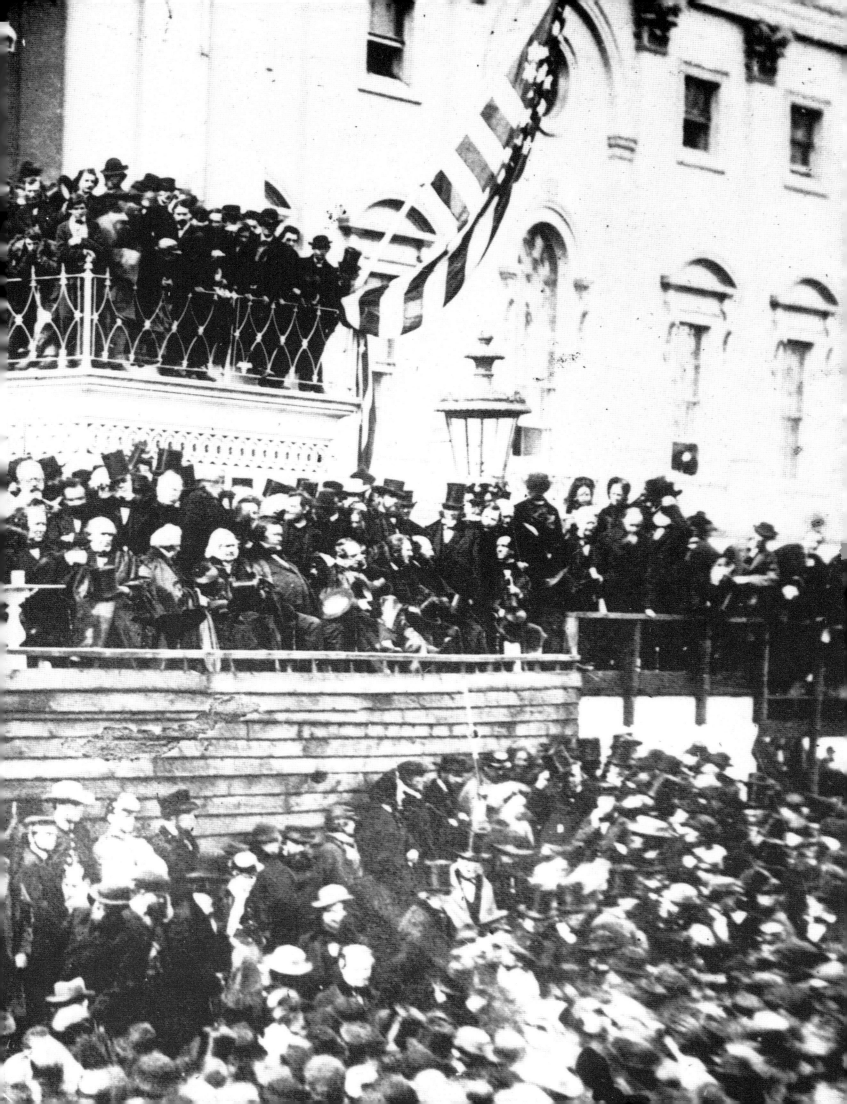

Previous pages: Lincoln delivers his second inaugural address. Lincoln noted that Northerners and Southerners worshipped the same God and that "each invokes His aid against the other." "It may seem strange that any man should dare to ask a just God's assistance" in support of slavery, Lincoln said but added: "let us judge not, that we be not judged." He hoped the war would soon end, but "if God wills that it continue until all the wealth piled by the bondman's 250 years of unrequited toil shall be sunk and until every drop of blood drawn with the lash shall be paid by another drawn with the sword," then the country must accept its fate.

Above: Freed slaves cheer Lincoln as he passes through Richmond on April 3. "I know I am free," said one black man, "for I have seen Father Abraham and felt him."

Left and opposite, top left: John Wilkes Booth leaps on to the stage of the Ford Theater after shooting Lincoln.

Opposite, bottom left: The house on 10th Street where Lincoln died after the attack.

Opposite, right: A notice of rewards offered for the capture of Booth and two of his accomplices, John H. Surratt and David C. Herold (here misspelled).

SURRAT. BOOTH. HAROLD.

War Department, Washington, April 20, 1865,

$100,000 REWARD!

THE MURDERER

Of our late beloved President, Abraham Lincoln,

IS STILL AT LARGE.

$50,000 REWARD

Will be paid by this Department for his apprehension, in addition to any reward offered by Municipal Authorities or State Executives.

$25,000 REWARD

Will be paid for the apprehension of JOHN H. SURRATT, one of Booth's Accomplices.

$25,000 REWARD

Will be paid for the apprehension of David C. Harold, another of Booth's accomplices.

LIBERAL REWARDS will be paid for any information that shall conduce to the arrest of either of the above-named criminals, or their accomplices.

All persons harboring or secreting the said persons, or either of them, or aiding or assisting their concealment or escape, will be treated as accomplices in the murder of the President and the attempted assassination of the Secretary of State, and shall be subject to trial before a Military Commission and the punishment of DEATH.

Let the stain of innocent blood be removed from the land by the arrest and punishment of the murderers.

All good citizens are exhorted to aid public justice on this occasion. Every man should consider his own conscience charged with this solemn duty, and rest neither night nor day until it be accomplished.

EDWIN M. STANTON, Secretary of War.

DESCRIPTIONS.—BOOTH is Five Feet 7 or 8 inches high, slender build, high forehead, black hair, black eyes, and wears a heavy black moustache.

JOHN H. SURRAT is about 5 feet, 9 inches. Hair rather thin and dark; eyes rather light; no beard. Would weigh 145 or 150 pounds. Complexion rather pale and clear, with color in his cheeks. Wore light clothes of fine quality. Shoulders square; cheek bones rather prominent; chin narrow; ears projecting at the top; forehead rather low and square, but broad. Parts his hair on the right side; neck rather long. His lips are firmly set. A slim man.

DAVID C. HAROLD is five feet six inches high, hair dark, eyes dark, eyebrows rather heavy, full face, nose short, hand short and fleshy, feet small, instep high, round bodied, naturally quick and active, slightly closes his eyes when looking at a person.

NOTICE.—In addition to the above, State and other authorities have offered rewards amounting to almost one hundred thousand dollars, making an aggregate of about TWO HUNDRED THOUSAND DOLLARS.

Opposite: The hanging of the assassination conspirators.

Above: The cover of sheet music for the "National Funeral March," in honor of Lincoln. Walt Whitman was another of the many American artists who paid tribute to Lincoln after his death and who felt keenly the irony of mourning and celebrating victory at the same time. "Exult O shores, and ring O bells! But I with mournful tread, Walk the deck my Captain lies, Fallen cold and dead."

Far left: Lincoln's hearse.

Below: Lincoln's funeral train.

Left: Lincoln's hearse passes beneath an arch at 12th Street in Chicago, Illinois, on May 1, 1865.

EPILOGUE: THE STRUGGLE OVER RECONSTRUCTION

The Union's victory gave the country's leaders an extraordinary opportunity both to establish new national standards of justice and equality and to pave the way for blacks to enter the mainstream of American life. "The conquerer has the right to make the terms, and we must submit," said one South Carolinian, expressing a common attitude that reflected a Southern concept of honor. But even as many Southerners stood ready to accept the consequences of defeat, the new President of the United States — a Tennessee native who had defiantly backed the Union during the war — refused to consider progressive reforms that would radically alter the racial hierarchy of Southern society.

A month after the surrender at Appomattox, President Andrew Johnson outlined his conditions for Reconstruction: Southern states would have only to repudiate secession, abolish slavery, and abrogate the Confederate debt. Beyond that, they were free to establish new legislatures and implement public policies as they saw fit.

The new Southern legislatures, encouraged by Johnson's leniency, acted quickly to restore some semblance of the antebellum social order. New laws, known as Black Codes, were enacted in an effort to maintain the inferior status of blacks. Such codes stipulated, for example, that unemployed blacks would be classified as vagrants and could be involuntarily hired out to white landowners. The codes also barred blacks from serving on juries and called for blacks convicted of certain crimes to be punished more severely than whites convicted of the same offenses.

The passage of such laws reinforced a belief among many Republican Congressmen that Johnson's policy was grossly inadequate, and in 1866 they passed a civil rights bill designed to counteract the reactionary movement in the South. The bill stipulated that all Americans, regardless of race, were citizens and were thus entitled to equal protection under the law. Congress also endorsed another bill extending the life of the Freedmen's Bureau, the agency created to provide basic needs to former slaves. Johnson refused to sign either bill, but Congress managed to override his vetoes. Subsequently, the lawmakers passed the 14th Amendment, which went still farther in guaranteeing due process and other rights to all citizens, regardless of race. To be sure, getting the amendment ratified proved more difficult: the amendment would not become part of the Constitution for another two years.

By 1867 the Republicans had become convinced that true social and political reform in the South would require measures far more drastic than those already taken. They consequently rammed through Congress the first Reconstruction Act, which divided the South into military districts and paved the way for new state constitutions. These constitutions ultimately gave blacks the right to vote and disqualified former Confederate leaders from holding office. Reacting to this new form of Federal "tyranny," many Southern whites boycotted subsequent state elections, and the political landscape throughout the region changed dramatically as a result.

Left: In February 1868 the House of Representatives voted to impeach President Andrew Johnson for "high crimes and misdemeanors." Pictured here is the impeachment committee in March 1868.

The state legislatures that subsequently emerged were supported and controlled by two key groups in addition to the newly empowered blacks: "scalawags" and the infamous "carpetbaggers."

Traditionally, the carpetbaggers have been depicted as cynically opportunistic Northerners who went south to manipulate the Reconstruction process for their own financial and political gain. Horace Greeley, for instance, said they had "crawled down South in the track of our armies, generally at a safe distance," while Woodrow Wilson later suggested they had used "the negroes as tools for their own selfish ends." Recent scholarship, particularly that of American historian Richard Nelson Current, suggests a somewhat different picture. While the backgrounds of the carpetbaggers varied widely, many of them had served with distinction in the Union army. While some undoubtedly were penniless adventurers who had little to offer society, others were highly educated men who brought considerable sums of money with them and invested it in the recovering region. Finally, while many were elected to political office, many others went South well before blacks were given the right to vote and thus had little hope of gaining political power at the time of their migration.

The scalawags were, for the most part, non-slaveholding Southerners who had remained loyal to the Union throughout the war. The emergence of Reconstruction had given them new power, and they wanted to keep the old Southern aristocrats from regaining their former status. Naturally, former Rebels hated the scalawags as much as they despised the carpetbaggers – perhaps more so, because they were viewed as traitors to the South.

Influential as these two groups were in shaping the South's political landscape in the aftermath of the war, blacks constituted a force that was even more potent. During the course of Reconstruction 16 blacks were elected to Congress, while hundreds held office on state and local levels. Contrary to popular perception, these black leaders were not ignorant puppets under the control of Northern whites. Most of them were relatively educated men who were not only trying to improve their own positions in life but those of their fellow black Americans as well. If a few of them were, in fact, unqualified for the offices they held, the same could easily be said of many white legislators.

Initially the Reconstruction governments did manage to advance the cause of justice and equality in the South through the passage of anti-discrimination laws, the establishment of public schools, and other measures. But Reconstruction lacked one key element: a comprehensive program of land reform. The Freedmen's Bureau had instituted piecemeal reforms by granting or leasing some abandoned lands to ex-slaves. But more sweeping programs either lacked support or proved ineffective. In the fall of 1865 Thaddeus Stevens proposed that land be confiscated from wealthy Southerners. Confiscation, he argued, would have two benefits: the land could be granted to freedmen, in 40-acre parcels, while the Southern elite would be forced "to labor, and teach their children to enter the workshop and handle the plow, and you will thus humble these proud traitors." Stevens failed to rally enough support for this harsh proposal, but in June of 1866 Congress did attempt to create a more moderate land reform program. The Southern Homestead Act set aside millions of acres across the South for individual grants. Settlers would be required to cultivate the land for five years, and it would then be theirs. But though some ex-slaves benefitted from the program, it was largely a failure because most freedmen lacked the capital to cultivate the land.

The limited scope of these economic reforms notwithstanding, conservative Southerners naturally felt threatened by them. Equally unsettling was the prospect of former slaves gaining political power. To combat these changes, white Southerners resorted to intimidation and violence, the main proponents of these tactics being the members of the infamous Ku Klux Klan.

In 1866 a group of Tennesseans had formed the Klan as a social club, but a year later former Rebel cavalry leader Nathan Bedford Forrest took control of it and changed it into a terrorist organization. Soon residents of other Southern states were banding together in similar groups, and for the next five years or so the Klan operated virtually without restraint.

But even as some local Republican governments were under siege, Republicans in Washington were solidifying their power. In 1868 the House of Representatives impeached President Johnson for attempting to remove Secretary of War Edwin M. Stanton. (The Representatives argued that Johnson had violated the Tenure of Office Act.) The Senate ultimately acquitted Johnson, but so narrowly that he lost his ability to function effectively as President. A few months later Ulysses S. Grant became the first elected President in post-war America.

Two years after taking office the Grant Administration struck hard at the Ku Klux Klan with new legislation and heightened enforcement. Congress, meanwhile, had passed the 15th Amendment, which guaranteed black suffrage. But these measures would prove to be among the last important achievements of the Reconstruction era.

A depressed economy in 1873 fostered a more conservative mood in Washington and around the country, and Democrats gradually began regaining power. By 1876 the Democrats had reasserted their supremacy throughout the South, taking control of legislatures in all but three states. During that Presidential election year the Democrats came out in full force, bringing the race between Rutherford B. Hayes and Samuel J. Tilden down to the wire. A dispute over the actual outcome of the election was resolved when the Democrats agreed to acknowledge the Republican Hayes as the winner in exchange for the removal of Reconstruction governments from those states that still had them.

In the wake of Reconstruction state and local governments throughout the South passed laws that largely reversed the civil rights reforms of the previous decade. While there was no hope of reviving the institution of slavery, Southerners nevertheless found ways of barring blacks from the political process and preventing them from establishing any kind of economic base. In this way they solidified a racial caste system that was all too reminiscent of the antebellum era, a system they managed to preserve for more than 80 years.

The 14th Amendment defined American citizens as "All persons born or naturalized in the United States" and went on to stipulate that "no State shall make or enforce any law which shall abridge the privileges or immunities of citizens of the United States." In so far as the 14th Amendment can be regarded as a logical expression of what had come to be, by the end of the Civil War, an important war aim of the North, it is clear that the victory of 1865 would remain uncompleted for the remainder of the century. Whether it has truly been completed today is moot.

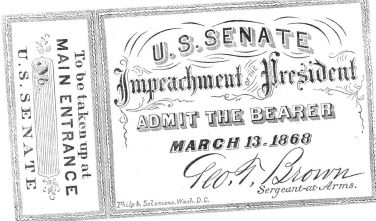

Opposite: President Andrew Johnson.

Left: T. Brown, sergeant-at-arms of the Senate, serves Johnson with a summons.

Below: The Senate impeachment proceedings.

Above right: A facsimile of an admission ticket to Johnson's impeachment trial.

Overleaf: A Union officer tries to hold off an angry white mob bent on attacking blacks at a Freedman's Bureau in the South.

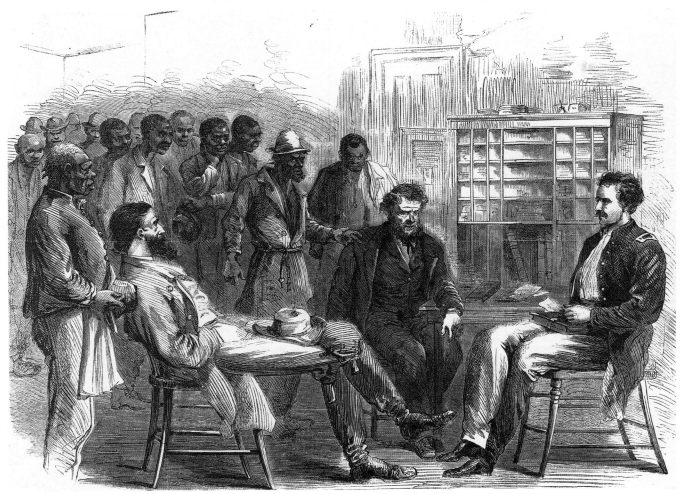

Opposite, top: Black soldiers prepare to leave Little Rock, Arksansas, shortly after the end of the war.

Opposite, bottom: Former slaves gather in the office of the Freedmen's Bureau in Memphis.

Above: ''The first vote,'' illustration from *Harper's Weekly* in November 1867.

Above: Black members of the 41st and 42nd Congresses, seated from left: Senator H.R. Revels of Mississippi; Representatives Benjamin Turner of Alabama: Josiah T. Walls of Florida; Joseph H. Rainy of Carolina; R. Brown Elliot, both of South Carolina; standing are Representatives Robert C. DeLarge of South Carolina and Jefferson H. Long of Georgia.

Left: Nathan B. Forrest, an organizer of the Ku Klux Klan.

Opposite: Federal troops occupy the state capitol in South Carolina in 1876.

Opposite, top: Armed Ku Klux Klan terrorists enter a black home.

Opposite, bottom: A night raid of the Ku Klux Klan.

Above: Klansmen prepare to lynch John Campbell in 1871.

INDEX

304

Acknowledgments

The publisher would like to thank David Eldred for designing this book, the Brompton Picture Research Department for obtaining the illustrations and Florence Norton for preparing the index.

Picture Credits

All pictures are from the Library of Congress and National Archives unless listed below: (T = top, B = bottom; L = left; R = right; C = center)

Bettmann Archive: 6, 8BL, 10T, 10BL, 21BR, 21T, 23BR, 25T, 26T, 28B, 29B, 32, 33T, 33CL, 33BR, 34, 35T, 35BR, 36TL, 36TR, 37TR, 37BL, 38TR, 38TL, 38BL, 39, 40TL, 40B, 41T, 41BR, 42TL, 42BL, 42BR, 43T, 43TR, 44-45TR, 44C, 45TR, 45B, 46T, 46-47B, 47TR, 47BR, 48T, 48BL, 49, 50TR, 50-51B, 51T, 53B, 56, 57T, 57BR, 58T, 58B, 59T, 59BR, 62, 66, 67T, 67B, 68T, 69T, 75, 76B, 77BR, 78B, 88B, 89T, 89CL, 89CR, 90T, 90B, 110, 111T, 111CL, 111CR, 112-113T, 113TR, 113BR, 134T, 135T, 140T, 146, 147T, 148T, 148BL, 162, 172, 173T, 173T, 173B, 180, 181, 182, 183, 184, 185, 186, 187BL, 187T, 194B, 195, 196B, 196TC, 197TR, 197B, 198, 199, 205T, 205CR, 207B, 209C, 230BR, 236T, 236BL, 239TC, 266, 267, 270, 271B, 272B, 274TL, 274BL, 275, 276T, 279TL, 281TL, 290, 291TL, 292-293, 297, 298, 299
Bloom Picture Library: 190TR
Brompton Picture Library: 9, 25BR, 30TR, 61T, 61BR, 64-65TL, 72-73, 74, 78TR, 81T, 81B, 84-85TR, 86C, 93BL, 96TL, 98-99BR, 103TR, 114T, 116B, 121B, 136B, 138B, 140B, 142BL, 142BR, 142-143T, 145T, 157B, 160B, 164B, 255B, 260CR, 260B, 263C, 264T, 268-269TC, 277
Anne S.K. Brown Military Collection, Brown University: 17T, 22T, 53T, 63BR, 78T, 80CR, 95T, 102TL, 102-103, 116T, 118-119T, 123TR, 122-123B, 141B, 148BR, 149T, 151T, 153T, 156T, 156B, 160T, 165B, 178T, 208B, 211T, 212B, 226, 227C, 230T, 235T, 250B, 251T, 253T, 254, 255TR, 261TR, 269CL, 281TR
Chicago Historical Society: 91BC, 100T, 158T, 163T, 170B, 174B, 175T
Hayes Presidential Center: 207T
Museum of the Confederacy: 98TL, 126B, 128-129T, 150T, 154-155B
Lincoln Library and Museum: 285TL
New York Historical Society: 189TR
New York Public Library: 97B, 100B, 128C, 171B
Norfolk Southern Corp.: 190B, 190CR
Railroad Museum of Pennsylvania: 288-289B
Smithsonian Institution: 30TL
Springfield Armory: 54BR, 55T
U.S. Naval Historical Center: 256TL, 264B, 265TL
Virginia Military Institute: 159T
Virginia State Library: 83CL, 83CR, 103TC